Southern Living.

The SOUTHERN HERITAGE COOKBOOK LIBRARY

The SOUTHERN HERITAGE
Sporting
Scene
COOKBOOK

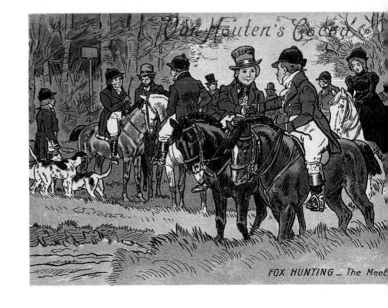

FOX HUNTING – The Meet

OXMOOR HOUSE
Birmingham, Alabama

Southern Living ®

The Southern Heritage Cookbook Library

Copyright 1985 by Oxmoor House, Inc.
Book Division of Southern Progress Corporation
P.O. Box 2463, Birmingham, Alabama 35201

Southern Living® is a federally registered trademark belonging to
Southern Living, Inc.

Library of Congress Catalog Number: 85-71901
ISBN: 0-8487-0618-8

Manufactured in the United States of America

The Southern Heritage SPORTING SCENE Cookbook

Executive Editor: Ann H. Harvey
Southern Living® *Foods Editor:* Jean W. Liles
Senior Editor: Joan E. Denman
Senior Foods Editor: Katherine M. Eakin
Assistant Editor: Ellen de Lathouder
Assistant Foods Editor: Helen R. Turk
Director, Test Kitchen: Laura N. Massey
Test Kitchen Home Economists: Kay E. Clarke, Rebecca J. Riddle,
   Elizabeth J. Taliaferro, Dee Waller, Elise Wright Walker
Production Manager: Jerry R. Higdon
Copy Editor: Melinda E. West
Editorial Assistants: Mary Ann Laurens, Donna A. Rumbarger,
   Karen P. Traccarella
Food Photographer: Jim Bathie
Food Stylist: Sara Jane Ball
Layout Designer: Christian von Rosenvinge
Mechanical Artist: Faith Nance
Research Editors: Alicia Hathaway, Philip Napoli

Special Consultants

Art Director: Irwin Glusker
Heritage Consultant: Meryle Evans
Foods Writer: Lillian B. Marshall
Food and Recipe Consultants: Marilyn Wyrick Ingram,
   Audrey P. Stehle

Cover: The Football Tailgate Picnic (page 124) is sure to satisfy hearty
pre-game appetites.

CONTENTS

Introduction 7

Equestrian Events 9

Hunter's Choice 39

The Great Escape 67

The Water's Edge 87

On the Green 109

Acknowledgments 138   Index 140

*Getting it right for the Savannah races:
strawberries and raspberries in Chilled Custard
served with Almond Lace Cookies and champagne
are only part of the fashionable
picnic menu that begins on page 64.*

INTRODUCTION

A Southerner who does not engage in some form of sport, if only as a spectator, is difficult to find. Pride in his own physical strength and in the speed of his horse were bred into the colonial man. Inactivity was alien to his nature. He worked at breeding perfection into his horses, organized the hunt, and then welcomed Irish steeplechasing.

By the end of the pioneer period, there were several race courses in middle Tennessee, with racing at Nashville and sweepstakes racing at Gallatin. Years after the Easterners had formalized the hunt, with red coats and ceremony that were most English, frontiersmen were hunting spontaneously, but with equal vigor, betting, and toast drinking.

Honed and refined, these were the sports and participants that eventuated into the elegant equestrian events of today's South: the steeplechase, polo, point-to-point, and the hunt—all date back to the sports-loving colonists and the equally hard-playing, hard-betting frontiersmen. Laws against excessive gambling were largely ignored.

As long as deer and elk were plentiful in the land drained by the Cumberland, they were hunted with dogs. Hunting is possible without a horse, but a hunter without a dog is in deep trouble if he's going for quail, dove, or duck. He'll pay all outdoors for a fine dog and take pride in training it, according to its breed, to point, set, retrieve. . . . Then he'll show it off at the drop of a hat and perhaps even dream of entering it in the National Field Trial Championship.

Those Southerners who lived near salt water evolved entertainments such as oyster roasts and sailing, while to their inland counterparts on rivers and lakes, boating, swimming, and especially fishing were prime amusements—all accompanied, certainly, by appropriate picnic foods. The competitive side of the Southerner shows often, whether it be as a spectator at the football field or as a participant on the tennis court. He also competes with himself: biking, hiking, fishing, and camping.

Good food, informally served, has always played an important role in the sporting scene. A bike ride in the country requires sustenance as surely as does a game of croquet. Have you noticed? Spectators get just about as hungry as the athletes themselves!

EQUESTRIAN EVENTS

MENU OF MENUS

CAROLINA CUP ELEGANCE

BURGOO TRADITION AT KEENELAND

SPECTATOR SPECIAL AT OAKLAWN

POINT-TO-POINT PICNIC AT WINTERTHUR

TANGLEWOOD HOSPITALITY

BELLE MEADE HUNT BREAKFAST

MARYLAND RING TOURNAMENT AND PICNIC

POLO PICNIC AT ROSE HILL PLANTATION

XIT RODEO AND REUNION BARBECUE

FORT WORTH EXPOSITION FARE

Elegance is the only word for it! All from the Carolina Cup menu: Caviar Ring, Marinated Beef Tenderloin, Herbed Mushrooms, Dressed Asparagus, and champagne.

The dedicated horse lover probably should migrate to the South—if he isn't already there. For it is entirely possible for him to involve himself in an equestrian event of one sort or another the year 'round. In his pursuit, he will travel Arkansas to Delaware, Kentucky to Texas, with stops in nigh every state in between.

The Dixie Circuit alone affords six weeks of thoroughbred racing in the Southeast, including Camden and Aiken, South Carolina; Atlanta, Georgia; and in North Carolina: Tryon, Southern Pines, and Clemmons. One must, of course, get to Lexington, Kentucky, for the spring meet at Keeneland. The Keeneland sales are as exciting as the racing; horse fanciers come from every state and abroad for the thoroughbred auctions.

The long tradition of the hunt prevails from November until March in many of the Southern states, and it carries many rituals dear to the participants. Equally revered is the Irish-born sport of steeplechasing. Originally the course included natural obstacles of brush, fences, and ditches. Now steeplechasers may race over hurdles of cedar or artificial materials, obstacles of timber posts and rails, or brush. A good steeplechaser is able to leap some twenty feet, cover a two-mile brush or hurdle course in less than four minutes or a four-mile course over timber or big brush in eight or nine minutes—all with electrifying grace and beauty.

Nineteenth-century Marylanders and Virginians were often "respectfully solicited" by formal invitations to attend ring tournaments. The jousts were brilliant social events in which young men of fashion tested their skills against the ancient rules of chivalry.

Polo, the oldest team sport, is relatively new to the South. But polo matches at Rose Hill Plantation in South Carolina already attract mobs of well-provendered tailgaters.

Like the polo match, a rodeo may not have the same following as racing or steeplechasing, but both are packed with action. The horses, while different, share an intuitive lightning response to their riders. What every equestrian event does have in common is this: excitement makes people hungry. Here are some ways for spectators to feast away their time after the trophies have been presented.

CAROLINA CUP ELEGANCE

"It's the biggest cocktail party in South Carolina," says one veteran trainer describing the Carolina Cup Steeplechase at Camden. Racing had lain dormant since the late 1800s, when some residents of Camden with members of the Camden Hunt Club began a movement in the 1920s to bring back steeplechasing. Today, on the Springdale Course, where many distinguished horses have trained and raced, throngs of fans gather for the Carolina Cup, a thrilling three-mile race over timber. The picnics unfurled there rival the elegant meals the fans enjoy at home; caviar and tenderloin lose none of their flavor served in the shade from a Mercedes.

HORSESHOE CHEESE MOLD
CAVIAR RING
HERBED MUSHROOMS
MARINATED BEEF TENDERLOIN
TUNA-RICE SALAD
DRESSED ASPARAGUS
CHEESE STRAWS
ASSORTED PICKLES AND RELISHES
AMARETTO MOUSSE
MONOGRAMMED PETITS FOURS
CHAMPAGNE

Serves 8

HORSESHOE CHEESE MOLD

1 pound mild Cheddar cheese, shredded
1 pound sharp Cheddar cheese, shredded
1 pound extra-sharp Cheddar cheese, shredded
1 cup mayonnaise
1 small onion, grated
1 teaspoon crushed red pepper
Fresh parsley sprigs
Melba toast

Combine all ingredients, except parsley and melba toast; mix well. Chill. Shape mixture into a horseshoe on a serving platter. Garnish with parsley. Serve with melba toast. Yield: 8 servings.

Horseshoe Cheese Mold triples the Cheddar and lays on some subtle flavors to make a delectable dish.

CAVIAR RING

8 hard-cooked eggs, finely
  chopped
½ cup mayonnaise
½ cup commercial sour
  cream
1 (7-ounce) jar black caviar,
  drained and rinsed
½ cup chopped green onion
3 (6-ounce) jars marinated
  artichoke hearts, drained
  and chopped
Assorted crackers

Press chopped eggs in the bottom of a lightly greased 4½-cup ring mold.

Combine mayonnaise and sour cream in a small mixing bowl, stirring well. Spread ½ cup of mayonnaise mixture evenly over eggs in mold; cover and refrigerate remaining mixture. Sprinkle three-fourths of caviar evenly over mayonnaise mixture in mold; cover and refrigerate remaining caviar. Sprinkle onion over caviar; press artichokes into mayonnaise mixture in mold. Cover and refrigerate overnight.

Unmold ring onto a serving platter. Spread reserved mayonnaise mixture over surface of ring; sprinkle with reserved caviar. Serve with assorted crackers. Yield: 8 servings.

HERBED MUSHROOMS

1 pound fresh mushrooms,
  cleaned and divided
1 tablespoon salt, divided
1 tablespoon sugar, divided
2 tablespoons finely chopped
  onion, divided
2 cloves garlic, minced and
  divided
¼ teaspoon white pepper,
  divided
¼ teaspoon crushed red
  pepper, divided
¼ teaspoon ground oregano,
  divided
2 cups red wine vinegar,
  divided
2 cups vegetable oil,
  divided

Place half of mushrooms in a quart jar. Add 1½ teaspoons salt, 1½ teaspoons sugar, 1 tablespoon onion, 1 clove garlic, ⅛ teaspoon white pepper, ⅛ teaspoon red pepper, ⅛ teaspoon oregano, 1 cup vinegar, and 1 cup oil. Cover and shake to mix well. Repeat procedure with remaining ingredients in a separate jar. Refrigerate overnight. Serve with a slotted spoon. Yield: 8 servings.

Note: Herbed Mushrooms may be prepared up to 1 week ahead of time.

MARINATED BEEF TENDERLOIN

1 (3-pound) beef tenderloin,
  trimmed
¼ cup butter
¼ cup Worcestershire sauce
1 tablespoon lemon juice
1 teaspoon meat and gravy
  browning and seasoning
  sauce
Fresh parsley sprigs (optional)

Place tenderloin in a 13- x 9- x 2-inch baking dish; set aside.

Combine remaining ingredients, except parsley, in a small saucepan; bring to a boil. Pour over tenderloin; cover and marinate overnight in refrigerator.

Place tenderloin on a rack in a shallow roasting pan, reserving marinade. Tuck narrow end under to make roast more uniformly thick. Insert meat thermometer, if desired.

Bake, uncovered, at 450° for 40 minutes or until meat thermometer registers 140° (rare); baste with marinade.

Cut tenderloin into 1-inch slices. Arrange on a warm serving platter. Garnish with parsley, if desired. Yield: 8 servings.

Horse and jockey silks are always attention getters: early 1900s trade card for Liebig Beef Extract.

Owners and jockeys attend to last minute details before the 1934 Carolina Cup race.

TUNA-RICE SALAD

3 cups chicken broth
1½ cups uncooked regular rice
2 (7-ounce) cans chunk white tuna, drained
1½ cups coarsely chopped unpeeled apple
1½ cups diced celery
½ cup chopped green onion
½ cup slivered toasted almonds
¼ cup raisins
½ cup mayonnaise
½ cup plain yogurt
2 tablespoons chutney
2 teaspoons curry powder

Bring chicken broth to a boil in a medium saucepan; add rice. Reduce heat; cover and cook 20 minutes or until rice is tender and liquid is absorbed. Chill thoroughly.

Combine remaining ingredients in a large mixing bowl; mix well. Add chilled rice; toss gently. Serve chilled. Yield: 8 servings.

DRESSED ASPARAGUS

1 cup water
1 cup vinegar
2 cups sugar
4 (3-inch) sticks cinnamon
12 whole cloves
2 teaspoons salt
2 teaspoons celery seeds
3 (15-ounce) cans white asparagus spears

Combine all ingredients, except asparagus, in a small saucepan; bring to a boil. Remove from heat; cool slightly.

Arrange asparagus in a shallow dish; pour marinade over asparagus. Cover and chill several hours. Drain; discard marinade. Yield: 8 servings.

CHEESE STRAWS

2 cups butter or margarine, softened
4 cups all-purpose flour, divided
1 teaspoon salt
1 teaspoon dry mustard
½ teaspoon red pepper
8 cups (2 pounds) shredded extra sharp Cheddar cheese

Cream butter in a large mixing bowl; set aside.

Combine flour, salt, mustard, and pepper in a large mixing bowl; mix well. Add 2 cups flour mixture to butter; beat well. Gradually add cheese; beat well. Add remaining flour mixture; beat well.

Press dough onto greased baking sheets, using a cookie press fitted with a star disc. Bake at 350° for 10 minutes or until lightly browned. Store in airtight containers, placing waxed paper between layers. Yield: about 15 dozen.

Note: Cheese Straws may be frozen in airtight containers.

AMARETTO MOUSSE

4 eggs, separated
1¼ cups milk
1 envelope unflavored gelatin
¼ cup plus 1 tablespoon cold
   water, divided
½ cup amaretto or other
   almond-flavored liqueur
½ cup sugar
1 cup sliced almonds, toasted
Dash of salt
1½ cups whipping cream
Whipped cream
Additional toasted sliced
   almonds

Beat egg yolks in a small mixing bowl until thick and lemon colored; add milk, stirring well. Pour yolk mixture into a medium saucepan; cook over medium heat, stirring constantly, 5 minutes or until thickened.

Soften gelatin in ¼ cup cold water; add to hot yolk mixture. Cook, stirring constantly, 2 minutes or until gelatin dissolves. Remove from heat; stir in amaretto. Pour hot mixture into a large mixing bowl. Chill to consistency of unbeaten egg white.

Combine sugar and remaining water in a small saucepan; cook over medium heat, stirring constantly, until sugar melts and turns light brown. Add 1 cup almonds, stirring to coat well. Quickly pour mixture on a sheet of aluminum foil. Cool. Break into small pieces. Stir pieces into congealed mixture.

Combine egg whites (at room temperature) and salt in a medium mixing bowl; beat until stiff peaks form. Fold into partially congealed mixture.

Beat 1½ cups whipping cream in a medium mixing bowl until soft peaks form. Fold into partially congealed mixture.

Spoon mixture into a 2-quart soufflé dish. Chill 4 hours or until set. Garnish with whipped cream and additional almonds. Spoon into individual serving bowls. Yield: 8 servings.

Mrs. T. H. Somerville
accepts the 1932 Carolina
Cup, a coveted victory.

MONOGRAMMED PETITS FOURS

1½ cups butter, softened
1 (8-ounce) package cream
   cheese, softened
3 cups sugar
6 eggs
3 cups all-purpose flour
½ teaspoon baking powder
1 teaspoon vanilla extract
1 teaspoon almond extract
Icing (recipe follows)
Royal Icing

Cream butter and cream cheese. Gradually add sugar, beating until light and fluffy. Add eggs, beating well.

Combine flour and baking powder; add to creamed mixture, beating at medium speed of an electric mixer 4 minutes. Stir in vanilla and almond extract. Pour into a heavily greased and floured 15- x 10- x 1-inch inch jellyroll pan. Bake at 325° for 50 minutes or until a wooden pick inserted in center comes out clean. Cool in pan 10 minutes. Remove to a wire rack, and cool completely.

Wrap cake in aluminum foil; freeze until firm. Cut cake into 1½-inch squares.

Drop squares, one at a time, into icing, turning to coat well; transfer to wire racks, using a fork. Let cakes dry. Monogram, as desired, with Royal Icing. Yield: about 5 dozen.

Icing:

2 (16-ounce) packages
   powdered sugar, sifted
¾ cup warm water
⅓ cup light corn syrup
1 teaspoon almond extract
Paste food coloring

Combine sugar, water, syrup, and almond extract; mix well. Tint to desired color with food coloring. Yield: icing for 5 dozen petits fours.

Royal Icing:

1 egg white
⅛ teaspoon cream of tartar
1 cup plus 3 tablespoons
   sifted powdered sugar

Combine egg white (at room temperature) and cream of tartar in a medium mixing bowl. Beat at medium speed of an electric mixer until foamy. Add sugar, 2 tablespoons at a time, beating at high speed of an electric mixer 5 minutes or until stiff peaks form.

Spoon icing into a pastry bag fitted with a round tip. Monogram petits fours, as desired. Yield: about ¾ cup.

BURGOO TRADITION AT KEENELAND

Keeneland, "the Saratoga of the South," near Lexington, Kentucky, began as a breeding farm and has kept that aura since opening as a track in 1936. In quiet country air, one hears the real sounds of racing: horses snorting and boots-to-saddle squeaking, as jockeys and mounts pass close to the clusters of people.

The multimillion-dollar obsession of thoroughbred breeding and racing finds its flowering at Keeneland. When appetites are ready for burgoo, Larry Wolken of Turf Catering Company dishes up the traditional track fare, just as his father, Keeneland's original caterer, did. The recipe goes back to the legendary "Burgoo King," Jim Looney.

OLD-FASHIONED KENTUCKY BURGOO
MIXED FRESH FRUIT
GREEN ONIONS
CORN STICKS
BREAD AND BUTTER PUDDING WITH BOURBON SAUCE

Serves 12

OLD-FASHIONED KENTUCKY BURGOO

1 (4-pound) stewing hen, quartered
1 pound pork shank
1 pound veal shank
1 pound beef shank
1 gallon water
3 medium potatoes, peeled and quartered
1 large onion, chopped
1 large green pepper, seeded and chopped
3 medium carrots, scraped and thinly sliced
1 cup thinly sliced okra
1 cup shredded cabbage
1 cup whole kernel corn
1 cup lima beans
1 cup chopped fresh parsley
½ cup finely chopped celery
1 red pepper pod
2 cups tomato puree
1 tablespoon salt
½ teaspoon red pepper
½ teaspoon hot sauce

Combine chicken, pork, veal, beef, and water in a large stockpot; bring to a boil. Reduce heat; cover and simmer 2 hours or until meat is tender.

Remove meat from broth; cool slightly. Remove meat from bones, discarding bones. Coarsely chop meat, and set aside.

Skim off, and discard fat from surface of broth. Add meat and remaining ingredients to broth in stockpot; bring to a boil. Reduce heat; simmer, uncovered, 6 hours or until thickened, stirring occasionally. Discard pepper pod.

Ladle stew into individual serving bowls; serve hot. Yield: about 3½ quarts.

Off and running from the starting gate at Keeneland, Lexington, Kentucky, 1946.

CORN STICKS

2 cups buttermilk
2 eggs, beaten
2 cups cornmeal
2 teaspoons baking powder
1 teaspoon salt
¼ teaspoon baking soda
3 tablespoons bacon drippings, divided

Combine buttermilk and eggs in a medium mixing bowl; mix well. Add cornmeal, baking powder, salt, and soda; stir well. Stir in 1 tablespoon plus 1½ teaspoons bacon drippings.

Brush cast-iron cornstick pans with remaining bacon drippings; heat in a 425° oven 3 minutes or until very hot. Spoon batter into pans, filling two-thirds full. Bake at 425° for 20 minutes or until golden brown. Yield: about 2 dozen.

Bread and Butter Pudding with Bourbon Sauce.

BREAD AND BUTTER PUDDING WITH BOURBON SAUCE

½ (16-ounce) loaf French bread, broken into 1-inch pieces
5½ cups milk, divided
¼ cup chopped pecans, toasted
½ cup butter or margarine, melted
8 eggs, beaten
2 cups sugar
1 teaspoon salt
1 teaspoon vanilla extract
Bourbon Sauce

Combine bread cubes and 2 cups milk in a large mixing bowl; let stand 5 minutes. Place mixture in a 12- x 8- x 2-inch baking dish; sprinkle with pecans. Pour melted butter over mixture. Toss gently.

Combine remaining milk, eggs, sugar, salt, and vanilla, mixing well; pour over bread mixture. Let stand 1 hour.

Place baking dish in a pan of warm water. Bake at 350° for 45 minutes or until a knife inserted in center comes out clean. Serve warm with Bourbon Sauce. Yield: 12 servings.

Bourbon Sauce:

1 cup butter or margarine
2 cups sifted powdered sugar
2 tablespoons (1 ounce) bourbon
2 eggs, beaten

Melt butter in top of a double boiler over simmering water. Add sugar and bourbon, stirring until sugar dissolves.

Gradually stir one-fourth of hot bourbon mixture into beaten eggs; add to remaining hot mixture in pan, stirring constantly. Cook, stirring constantly, 5 minutes or until mixture thickens. Serve hot. Yield: about 2 cups.

SPECTATOR SPECIAL
AT OAKLAWN

Oaklawn Park at Hot Springs, Arkansas, has been in business, off and on, since around 1904, when five men formed the Oaklawn Jockey Club. A descendant of two of the organizers, Charles Cella of St. Louis, still is active in building Oaklawn into a top racing facility. Among the state's leading breeders are Mr. and Mrs. Herman Udouj of Sundridge Farms, whose racing stock is based on two stallions from the Keeneland sales in Lexington, Kentucky. Spectators go for corned beef on rye at Oaklawn. Larry Wolken's father started catering at this track in 1936 and, being a Chicagoan, decided on corned beef. Folks called it "red ham" and ate it up. They still do, just as they go for the burgoo Larry Wolken purveys at Keeneland.

CORNED BEEF SANDWICHES
DARK RYE BREAD
MOLASSES SPICE BARS
BEER

Serves 12

*Steeplechasing rabbit
is about to hurdle
over a leafy hedge on
1890s trade card.*

CORNED BEEF
SANDWICHES

1 (3- to 4-pound) corned beef
   brisket
24 (⅜-inch-thick) slices Dark
   Rye Bread
24 slices tomato
24 lettuce leaves
12 slices Swiss cheese
¼ cup mayonnaise, divided
¼ cup mustard, divided
¼ cup prepared horseradish,
   divided

Place brisket and juices from
bag in a large Dutch oven with
cold water to cover; insert meat
thermometer into thickest part
of brisket, if desired. Bring to a
boil. Reduce heat; cover and
simmer 3½ hours or until brisket is tender or meat thermometer registers 180°. Remove
brisket from water; let stand 30
minutes. Cut into thin slices
diagonally across the grain.
Yield: 12 servings.

To Make Sandwiches: Place
corned beef on half of Dark Rye
Bread slices; top each with a tomato slice, a lettuce leaf, a
cheese slice, and a teaspoon
each of mayonnaise, mustard,
and horseradish. Cover with remaining bread slices.

*Corned Beef on rye bread
was caterer's special
at Oaklawn. Race fans
liked the "red ham."*

DARK RYE BREAD

3 to 4 cups all-purpose flour,
   divided
2 packages dry yeast
1 tablespoon sugar
2 cups warm water (105° to
   115°), divided
3 cups rye flour
¼ cup cocoa
1 tablespoon salt
1 tablespoon caraway seeds
⅓ cup molasses
2 tablespoons butter or
   margarine

Combine ½ cup all-purpose
flour, yeast, sugar, and ¾ cup
water; let stand 5 minutes.

Add remaining water, rye
flour, cocoa, salt, caraway
seeds, molasses, and butter to
yeast mixture; stir well. Add
enough remaining all-purpose
flour to make a soft dough. Turn
dough out onto a floured surface; knead 10 minutes or until
smooth and elastic. Place in a
greased bowl, turning to grease
top. Cover and let rise in a warm
place (85°), free from drafts, 1
hour or until doubled in bulk.

Punch dough down; divide in
half. Shape each half into a ball.
Place each ball in a greased 8-
inch round cakepan. Cover and
repeat rising procedure 1 hour
or until doubled in bulk.

Bake at 400° for 25 minutes
or until loaves sound hollow
when tapped. Remove from
pans; cool on wire racks. Yield:
2 loaves.

MOLASSES
SPICE BARS

3 egg yolks
1 egg
¾ cup sugar
1½ cups all-purpose flour
1 teaspoon baking powder
1½ teaspoons ground
   cinnamon
½ teaspoon ground allspice
½ teaspoon ground cloves
1 cup dark molasses
1 (1-ounce) square
   unsweetened chocolate
2 tablespoons butter or
   margarine
1 tablespoon plus 1 teaspoon
   bourbon
1 cup chopped pecans
Powdered sugar

Combine egg yolks, egg, and
¾ cup sugar in a medium mixing bowl; beat at medium speed
of an electric mixer until well
blended.

Combine flour, baking powder, and spices in a small mixing bowl; stir well. Gradually
add to egg mixture alternately
with molasses; beat well.

Cook chocolate and butter in
top of a double boiler over simmering water, stirring constantly, until mixture melts.
Add to batter, mixing well. Stir
in bourbon and pecans.

Spoon batter into a well-
greased 13- x 9- x 2-inch baking
pan. Bake at 325° for 30 minutes or until a wooden pick inserted in center comes out
clean. Cool in pan on a wire
rack. Sift powdered sugar over
cake, and cut into 3- x 1-inch
bars. Yield: about 3 dozen.

POINT-TO-POINT PICNIC AT WINTERTHUR

Point-to-point races originated in Ireland in the mid-1700s as cross-country steeplechases over natural obstacles. Today, the point-to-point at Winterthur Gardens near Wilmington, Delaware, is run over a flagged course of post-and-rail fence hurdles. Winterthur is on a circuit of such races which extends from Virginia to New York. The springtime event draws dressy tailgate picnickers, some of whom understand horses and racing. For some, it is enough that the azaleas and dogwoods are in bloom and that, given the setting and the quality of the food, a good time is a foregone conclusion. It would be hard to find more elaborate picnic fare.

WINTERTHUR PUNCH
BROCCOLI SOUP
LEMON CHICKEN BREASTS
MARINATED VEGETABLE SALAD
HERB BREAD
ORANGES IN WINE SAUCE
FRUITED ICED TEA

Serves 8

WINTERTHUR PUNCH

Orange slices
Lemon slices
Maraschino cherries
1 (750 ml) bottle Sauterne, chilled
1½ cups Cognac
1½ cups lemon juice
¾ cup Triple Sec or other orange-flavored liqueur
¾ cup grenadine
1 (23-ounce) bottle mineral water
Fresh mint sprigs (optional)

Pour water into a 9-cup ring mold to a depth of ¼-inch; freeze until firm. Arrange orange slices, lemon slices, and maraschino cherries on top of frozen layer. Pour ¾ cup cold water over top, and freeze. Continue adding ¾ cup cold water and freezing after each addition until mold is filled and completely frozen.

To serve, unmold ice ring, and place in a punch bowl. Combine Sauterne, Cognac, lemon juice, Triple Sec, and grenadine. Pour over ice ring. Gradually stir in mineral water. Garnish with mint sprigs, if desired. Yield: about 3 quarts.

BROCCOLI SOUP

4½ cups milk
2 (10-ounce) packages frozen chopped broccoli, cooked and drained
8 sprigs fresh parsley
¼ cup chopped celery leaves
¼ cup all-purpose flour
¼ cup butter or margarine, melted
2 thin slices onion
2 teaspoons salt
¼ teaspoon pepper
Additional celery leaves

Combine all ingredients, except additional celery leaves, in container of an electric blender; process until smooth. Pour mixture into top of a double boiler; cook over simmering water until thickened. Serve hot; garnish with additional celery leaves. Yield: about 7 cups.

LEMON CHICKEN BREASTS

¼ cup butter or margarine, melted
1 clove garlic, crushed
8 chicken breast halves, skinned and boned
½ cup Italian-style dry breadcrumbs
¼ cup freshly squeezed lemon juice
Lemon slices
Fresh parsley sprigs

Combine butter and garlic in an 8-inch square baking dish.

Flatten chicken with a meat mallet; fold envelope fashion, and roll in breadcrumbs.

Place chicken in baking dish, turning to coat well. Bake at 350° for 30 minutes, basting occasionally. Add lemon juice; bake an additional 15 minutes or until tender. Transfer chicken to individual serving plates. Garnish with lemon and parsley. Yield: 8 servings.

Lemon Chicken Breasts, Marinated Vegetable Salad; Herb Bread and Fruited Iced Tea (page 20).

Riders in this 1940s photograph overleap the hedges in a point-to-point race.

The Chronicle of the Horse

MARINATED VEGETABLE SALAD

2 (10-ounce) packages frozen green peas, thawed
1 (8-ounce) can water chestnuts, drained and diced
1 (6-ounce) can pitted ripe olives, drained
1 (4-ounce) jar sliced pimientos, drained
1 bunch green onions, sliced
2 cups sliced fresh mushrooms
French Dressing

Combine peas, water chestnuts, olives, pimientos, onions, and mushrooms in a 12- x 8- x 2-inch baking dish. Pour French Dressing over vegetable mixture; toss lightly. Cover and marinate in refrigerator at least 3 hours before serving. Yield: 8 servings.

French Dressing:

¼ cup plus 2 tablespoons olive oil
¼ cup red wine vinegar
1 tablespoon salt
½ teaspoon freshly ground black pepper
1 clove garlic, crushed

Combine all ingredients in a small jar. Cover and shake vigorously. Store in refrigerator. Yield: ½ cup.

HERB BREAD

2 cups milk, scalded
¼ cup sugar
¼ cup vegetable oil
1 tablespoon salt
¼ cup celery seeds
2 teaspoons rubbed sage
1 teaspoon ground nutmeg
2 packages dry yeast
½ cup warm water (105° to 115°)
2 eggs, beaten
7 cups all-purpose flour, divided

Combine first 7 ingredients in a large mixing bowl; cool to lukewarm (105° to 115°).

Dissolve yeast in warm water, stirring well; let stand 5 minutes or until bubbly.

Add dissolved yeast, eggs, and 3 cups flour to milk mixture; beat until smooth. Add remaining flour to form a soft dough.

Turn dough out onto a floured surface; knead 5 minutes or until smooth and elastic. Place dough in a greased bowl, turning to grease top. Cover and let rise in a warm place (85°), free from drafts, 1 hour or until doubled in bulk.

Punch dough down; turn out onto a lightly floured surface. Let rest 15 minutes. Divide dough into 2 equal portions; shape each portion into a round loaf. Place each loaf in a 9-inch round cakepan. Cover and repeat rising procedure 45 minutes or until doubled in bulk.

Bake at 400° for 15 minutes. Cover tops loosely with aluminum foil; bake an additional 20 minutes or until loaves sound hollow when tapped. Remove loaves from pans; cool on wire racks. Yield: 2 loaves.

ORANGES IN WINE SAUCE

8 oranges, peeled, sectioned, and seeded
1 cup Burgundy or other dry red wine
1 cup water
¾ cup sugar
2 slices lemon, seeded
3 whole cloves
½ teaspoon ground cinnamon

Place orange sections in a medium mixing bowl; set aside. Combine remaining ingredients in a small saucepan, stirring well. Bring to a boil; boil, stirring occasionally, until mixture is reduced by half. Remove and discard whole cloves. Pour hot sauce over reserved orange sections. Refrigerate until thoroughly chilled. Transfer to a serving bowl, and serve chilled. Yield: 8 servings.

FRUITED ICED TEA

2½ quarts water, divided
1½ cups sugar
12 regular tea bags
1 quart boiling water
2 cups orange juice
¾ cup lemon juice
Lemon slices

Combine 2 cups water and sugar in a small saucepan. Cook over medium heat, stirring frequently, until sugar dissolves and mixture comes to a boil; boil 5 minutes. Set aside.

Place tea bags in a 1-quart glass pitcher; slowly pour boiling water over tea bags. Cover and steep 15 minutes. Discard tea bags. Combine tea, reserved syrup, remaining water, and orange and lemon juice; stir until well blended. Chill.

Serve chilled tea over ice; garnish with lemon slices. Yield: about 1 gallon.

TANGLEWOOD HOSPITALITY

Just as the Carolina Cup Steeplechase opens the springfest they call the Dixie Circuit, Tanglewood, held at Clemmons, near Winston-Salem, North Carolina, concludes it. The event began in 1963 and is run on a 1,200-acre expanse which includes golf, tennis, and swimming facilities. Of course, the calendar is dotted with important steeplechases in other Southern states: Georgia, Maryland, Virginia, and Kentucky. But when they drop the tailgate on the final repast of the Dixie Circuit, that's it for many Eastern fans until steeplechasing picks up in the fall with the Fairfax event at Leesburg, Virginia. For an end-of-circuit gala, start with Mint Juleps.

MINT JULEPS
CHILLED PICKLED SHRIMP
HERB DIP WITH VEGETABLES
SPINACH BALLS
CHEESE DREAMS
STRAWBERRIES WITH RICH CREAM
PECAN ICEBOX COOKIES

Serves 12

MINT JULEPS

½ cup sugar
¼ cup water
17 sprigs fresh mint
Shaved ice
1 (1-liter) bottle Kentucky bourbon
Additional fresh mint sprigs

Combine sugar, water, and 17 mint sprigs in a small saucepan. Bring to a boil, stirring until sugar dissolves. Remove from heat. Strain and discard mint. Chill syrup several hours or overnight.

To serve, fill each julep cup three-fourths full with shaved ice; add 2 jiggers (¼ cup plus 2 tablespoons) bourbon and 1 teaspoon reserved syrup. Stir gently. Add additional shaved ice to fill cups. Garnish with additional mint sprigs. Yield: 12 servings.

Herb Dip with Vegetables (front), Chilled Pickled Shrimp, and Mint Juleps; that's hospitality plus.

Clearing the hedge in a steeplechase race, circa 1940.

CHILLED PICKLED SHRIMP

1 gallon water
½ cup celery leaves
1 lemon, sliced
¼ cup salt
2 tablespoons vinegar
1 teaspoon seasoned salt
1 teaspoon whole peppercorns
1 teaspoon Worcestershire sauce
1 teaspoon hot pepper sauce
½ teaspoon garlic salt
2½ pounds uncooked medium shrimp
1 medium onion, sliced and separated into rings
6 bay leaves
Dressing (recipe follows)

Combine first 10 ingredients in a large stockpot; stir well, and bring to a boil. Add shrimp, and cook 4 minutes. (Do not boil.) Drain and discard cooking liquid. Peel and devein shrimp.

Layer boiled shrimp, onion rings, and bay leaves in 2 wide-mouthed quart jars. Pour dressing evenly into each jar. Cover with metal lids, and screw bands tight. Chill 12 hours, inverting jars frequently. Drain

and discard bay leaves. Serve chilled shrimp on wooden picks. Yield: 12 appetizer servings.

Dressing:

1 cup vegetable oil
¾ cup vinegar
⅓ cup catsup
2 tablespoons celery seeds
1 tablespoon garlic salt
1½ teaspoons dry mustard
1½ teaspoons Worcestershire sauce

Combine all ingredients in a jar. Cover tightly, and shake vigorously. Yield: about 2 cups.

Trade card, circa 1890.

HERB DIP WITH VEGETABLES

1 cup cream-style cottage cheese
1 cup mayonnaise
½ cup commercial sour cream
3 tablespoons chopped fresh chives
2 tablespoons chopped fresh parsley
2 tablespoons grated onion
2 cloves garlic, minced
1 tablespoon sesame seeds
1 teaspoon Worcestershire sauce
½ teaspoon salt
½ teaspoon white pepper
¼ teaspoon hot sauce
Paprika
Raw vegetables

Combine cottage cheese, mayonnaise, and sour cream; beat at medium speed of an electric mixer until smooth. Add chives, parsley, onion, garlic, sesame seeds, Worcestershire sauce, salt, pepper, and hot sauce, mixing well. Spoon into a serving bowl; sprinkle with paprika. Chill. Serve with raw vegetables. Yield: about 3 cups.

SPINACH BALLS

1 (10-ounce) package frozen chopped spinach
1 cup seasoned stuffing mix
½ cup grated Parmesan cheese
3 eggs, beaten
3 tablespoons butter or margarine, softened
¼ teaspoon salt
⅛ teaspoon pepper

Cook spinach according to package directions, omitting salt; drain, pressing spinach.

Combine spinach and remaining ingredients in a medium mixing bowl; mix well. Shape into 1-inch balls, and place on a baking sheet. Freeze. Transfer frozen spinach balls to a plastic bag; store in freezer.

To serve, place frozen spinach balls on a baking sheet, and bake at 350° for 10 to 15 minutes. Yield: 2 dozen.

CHEESE DREAMS

4 cups all-purpose flour
½ teaspoon salt
1 teaspoon red pepper
4 cups (16 ounces) shredded sharp Cheddar cheese
2 cups butter or margarine, softened

Sift together flour, salt, and pepper; cut in cheese and butter with a pastry blender. Continue mixing until mixture forms a dough.

Turn dough out onto a lightly floured surface; roll to ¼-inch thickness. Cut with a 1½-inch biscuit cutter. Place 1 inch apart on ungreased baking sheets. Bake at 375° for 15 minutes or until crisp. Remove from baking sheets, and cool on wire racks. Yield: about 10 dozen.

STRAWBERRIES WITH RICH CREAM

1 quart vanilla ice cream, softened
2 cups whipping cream, whipped
¾ cup Triple Sec or other orange-flavored liqueur
¼ cup lemon juice
3 quarts fresh whole strawberries, washed and hulled

Beat ice cream in a large mixing bowl until smooth; fold in whipped cream. Add Triple Sec and lemon juice, stirring well. Serve immediately over strawberries in individual bowls. Yield: 12 servings.

PECAN ICEBOX COOKIES

1 cup butter, softened
2 cups sugar
3 eggs
3 cups all-purpose flour
2 teaspoons salt
1 teaspoon baking soda
2 tablespoons vanilla extract
1 cup chopped pecans

Cream butter in a large mixing bowl; add sugar, beating well. Add eggs; beat well.

Sift together flour, salt, and soda in a medium mixing bowl; add to creamed mixture, stirring well. Add vanilla and pecans, stirring well.

Divide dough in half; shape each half into a roll, 1½ inches in diameter. Wrap each roll in waxed paper; chill until firm.

Remove waxed paper, and cut rolls into ¼-inch-thick slices. Place 2 inches apart on lightly greased cookie sheets. Bake at 375° for 6 to 8 minutes or until lightly browned. Remove from cookie sheets, and cool on wire racks. Store in airtight containers. Yield: about 10 dozen.

Members of the Cow Horn Club get together to sip mint juleps in Richmond County, Georgia, circa 1901.

BELLE MEADE HUNT BREAKFAST

When the members of the Belle Meade Hunt of Thomson, Georgia, assemble at Hawes Hill on the first Saturday of November, about four hundred horse and tally-ho wagon riders, those who follow the hunt in wagons pulled by tractors, share the anticipation. Saturdays and Wednesdays, November through March, hunters, hounds, and horses range across 30,000 rolling acres to the music of the Huntsman's horn. The Foxes Den Supper that follows each hunt is hosted by a group of families; Belle Meade includes every family member in the sport. To end the season, the hunt begins early in the morning and is followed by a sumptuous breakfast. To cap it all: several hundred celebrants attend an evening reception followed by a dance.

BLOODY MARYS
BELLE MEADE SPECIALS
CHEESE GRITS
GINGER FRUIT CUPS
STRAWBERRY MUFFINS
SOUR CREAM GEMS
FRUIT PUNCH WITH ICE RING
COFFEE

Serves 12

BLOODY MARYS

1 (46-ounce) can tomato juice
1½ cups vodka
Juice of 6 limes
¼ cup Worcestershire sauce
¼ cup Pickapeppa sauce
¼ teaspoon hot sauce
1 tablespoon plus 1½ teaspoons salt
1½ teaspoons sugar
Crushed ice

Combine all ingredients, except ice, in a large pitcher; stir well. Chill thoroughly. Serve over crushed ice. Yield: 2 quarts.

BELLE MEADE SPECIALS

2 pounds bulk pork sausage
¼ cup plus 1 tablespoon water
12 poached eggs
Béarnaise Sauce
Fresh parsley sprigs

Shape sausage into 12 large patties. Place patties in a large, cool skillet; add water. Cover and cook over medium heat 5 minutes. Turn patties; continue cooking, uncovered, until browned. Drain well.

Place sausage patties on a large serving platter. Top each with a poached egg; cover with Béarnaise Sauce. Garnish with fresh parsley sprigs. Yield: 12 servings.

Béarnaise Sauce:

¾ cup Chablis or other dry white wine
3 tablespoons tarragon vinegar
3 tablespoons minced green onion
6 egg yolks
2¼ cups butter or margarine, melted
1 tablespoon plus 1½ teaspoons lemon juice
¼ teaspoon salt
¼ teaspoon white pepper
¼ teaspoon red pepper

Combine wine, vinegar, and onion in a small saucepan. Cook over medium heat 10 minutes or until liquid is reduced to ½ cup. Strain; discard onion. Cool slightly.

Beat egg yolks until thick and lemon colored. Gradually stir one-fourth of hot mixture into yolks; add to remaining hot mixture, stirring constantly. Cook, stirring constantly, until thickened. Remove from heat; stir in butter, 1 tablespoon at a time. Stir in remaining ingredients. Serve immediately. Yield: 3 cups.

24

Belle Meade Specials, Sour Cream Gems, and coffee.

FOX HUNTING — The Meet

Gathering for a fox hunt, 1890s trade card.

CHEESE GRITS

1½ cups uncooked regular grits
¾ cup butter or margarine
3 cups (12 ounces) shredded sharp Cheddar cheese
4 eggs, beaten
½ teaspoon Worcestershire sauce
¼ teaspoon garlic salt

Cook grits in a medium saucepan according to package directions. Remove from heat; add butter and cheese, stirring until cheese melts. Gradually add beaten eggs. Stir in Worcestershire sauce and garlic salt. Cook over medium heat, stirring until thoroughly heated. Yield: 12 servings.

GINGER FRUIT CUPS

1 fresh pineapple, peeled, cored, and cut into 1-inch pieces
6 large seedless oranges, peeled and sectioned
1 cup grated coconut
1 tablespoon finely chopped gingerroot
2 teaspoons grated orange rind
¾ cup orange juice
¼ cup Cointreau or other orange-flavored liqueur

Combine all ingredients; toss lightly. Cover and chill. Spoon into individual serving bowls. Yield: 12 servings.

STRAWBERRY MUFFINS

2 cups all-purpose flour
⅓ cup sugar
2 teaspoons ground cinnamon
1 teaspoon baking soda
½ teaspoon salt
1 (10-ounce) package frozen sliced strawberries, thawed and undrained
2 eggs, beaten
⅓ cup vegetable oil

Combine flour, sugar, cinnamon, soda, and salt in a large mixing bowl; make a well in center of mixture.
Chop strawberries; combine strawberries, eggs, and oil. Add to flour mixture, stirring until dry ingredients are moistened.
Spoon batter into greased miniature muffin pans, filling two-thirds full. Bake at 350° for 25 minutes or until golden brown. Yield: 3 dozen.

SOUR CREAM GEMS

2 cups self-rising flour
1 cup butter or margarine, softened
1 (8-ounce) carton commercial sour cream
Additional butter

Place self-rising flour in a medium mixing bowl. Cut in 1 cup butter with a pastry blender until mixture resembles coarse meal. Gradually add sour cream, stirring just until dry ingredients are moistened.
Spoon batter into lightly greased miniature muffin pans, filling two-thirds full. Bake at 400° for 20 minutes or until lightly browned. Serve warm with additional butter. Yield: about 3 dozen.

FRUIT PUNCH WITH ICE RING

1 (46-ounce) can unsweetened orange juice
1 quart unsweetened pineapple juice
1½ cups lemon juice
1 orange, thinly sliced
1 lemon, thinly sliced
1 (6-ounce) jar maraschino cherries, drained
3 quarts water
1½ cups sugar
1½ quarts ginger ale

Combine orange, pineapple, and lemon juice in a large container, stirring well. Pour 1 quart fruit juice mixture into a 6-cup ring mold, reserving remaining juice mixture. Arrange orange slices, lemon slices, and cherries attractively in mold. Freeze until ready to serve.
Combine water and sugar in a large mixing bowl, stirring until sugar dissolves. Add to reserved fruit juice mixture, stirring well. Chill thoroughly.
Pour chilled juice mixture over prepared ice ring in a large punch bowl; add ginger ale just before serving. Serve immediately. Yield: about 2 gallons.

MARYLAND RING TOURNAMENT AND PICNIC

I n 1804, ring tilting, or jousting, was introduced in Maryland via England. The game was an elaborate and colorful tournament that found a natural home in an environment already proven hospitable to equine sports. The game has since been proclaimed the official sport of Maryland. Riding at the ring consists of a rider, a quick horse, a lance, and a ring suspended nine feet above the ground. Today's version may have less pageantry, but the "knight" still has three tries at the ring and the chance to show off his horsemanship. As tilting has always made knights and ladies hungry, a well-stocked hamper is in order, cool beverages, too; tilting's hot work.

CHESAPEAKE BAY CRAB CAKE SANDWICHES
BAKED HAM SANDWICHES
STRAWBERRY SHORTCAKE
ICED TEA
BEER

Serves 12

Tournament fare: Chesapeake Bay Crab Cake Sandwiches and beer.

CRAB.

STRAWBERRY SHORTCAKE

2 quarts fresh strawberries,
  hulled and sliced
1½ cups sugar
Sweet Biscuits
2 cups whipping cream,
  whipped

Combine sliced strawberries and sugar; stir well. Let stand at least 30 minutes, allowing sugar to dissolve.

Split Sweet Biscuits in half, placing bottom halves on serving plates. Spoon half of strawberries evenly over biscuits, and replace tops. Spoon remaining strawberries evenly over tops; dollop with whipped cream. Serve immediately. Yield: 12 servings.

Sweet Biscuits:

2½ cups all-purpose flour
2 tablespoons sugar
1 tablespoon baking powder
1 teaspoon salt
⅓ cup shortening or butter
¾ cup milk
1 egg, beaten

Combine flour, sugar, baking powder, and salt in a medium mixing bowl. Cut in shortening with a pastry blender until mixture resembles coarse meal.

Combine milk and egg, stirring well; pour evenly over flour mixture, stirring until dry ingredients are moistened.

Turn dough out onto a lightly floured surface; knead lightly 3 or 4 times. Roll to 1-inch thickness; cut with a 2¼-inch biscuit cutter. Place biscuits on a lightly greased baking sheet. Bake at 425° for 12 minutes or until lightly browned. Yield: 1 dozen.

Note: Sweet Biscuits may be frozen until needed.

Plumed rider in tilting tournament at Horn Point, Maryland, 1886, takes dead aim at suspended ring. Then, "the successful knight presents the victor's wreath to the queen of beauty."

CHESAPEAKE BAY CRAB CAKE SANDWICHES

2 slices white bread
2 eggs, well beaten
¼ cup mayonnaise
2 teaspoons Worcestershire
  sauce
1 teaspoon salt
1 teaspoon dry mustard
¼ teaspoon red pepper
2 pounds claw crabmeat,
  drained and flaked
3 cups fine dry breadcrumbs
Vegetable oil
12 sandwich buns, split
Commercial tartar sauce

Place bread in a large mixing bowl with water to cover; let stand 5 minutes. Drain, squeezing excess water from bread; return to mixing bowl. Add eggs, mayonnaise, Worcestershire sauce, salt, mustard, and pepper; mix well. Fold in crabmeat.

Shape mixture into 12 patties; roll each in breadcrumbs. Fry in deep hot oil (350°) until golden brown, turning once. Drain on paper towels.

Place 1 crab cake in each bun. Serve warm with tartar sauce. Yield: 12 servings.

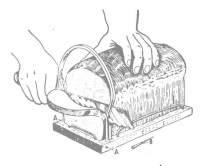

BAKED HAM SANDWICHES

1 (11- to 12-pound) country
  ham
1 tablespoon whole
  cloves
½ cup firmly packed brown
  sugar
2 teaspoons dry mustard
¼ cup all-purpose flour
2 tablespoons vinegar
24 slices white or rye bread,
  divided
Mustard
Mayonnaise

Place ham in a large container; cover with cold water, and soak overnight. Drain ham, and scrub thoroughly with a stiff brush; rinse well with cold water.

Return ham to container, and cover with fresh cold water. Bring to a boil. Reduce heat; simmer 2 hours and 45 minutes or 15 minutes per pound. Let cool slightly.

Carefully remove ham from water; remove skin. Place ham, fat side up, on a cutting board; score fat in a diamond pattern, and stud with whole cloves. Place ham, fat side up, in a shallow roasting pan.

Combine sugar, mustard, flour, and vinegar; mix well. Coat ham with mixture. Bake, uncovered, at 350° for 30 minutes, basting occasionally. Transfer to a serving platter; cool completely. Cut into thin slices. To make sandwiches, place several ham slices between 2 bread slices; spread with mustard and mayonnaise. Yield: 12 sandwiches.

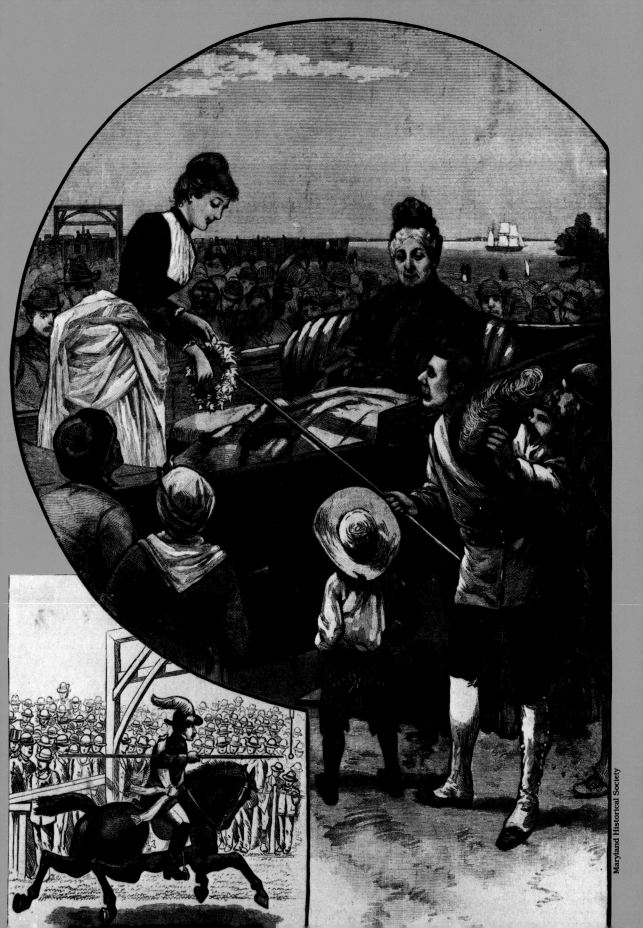

POLO PICNIC AT ROSE HILL PLANTATION

The Gothic Revival mansion at Rose Hill Plantation near Bluffton, South Carolina, is notable on two counts: the architectural style is rare in the South, and it was unscathed by the Civil War. Dr. John Kirk started construction in the 1850s, but it was many years before others completed it. Once an enormous cotton plantation, it was named in 1983 to the National Register of Historic Places and is now home to a splendid equestrian center on 3,300 acres. Polo, the Persian "ballgame on horseback" and the world's oldest team sport, came to Rose Hill in 1982. Tailgaters turn up with champagne and beautiful food to see the "sport of kings."

HERBED TOMATO CONSOMMÉ
COLD ROAST QUAIL WITH SAVORY ORANGE SAUCE
WALDORF SALAD WITH WINE
FRENCH BREAD
HOT SPICED COMPOTE
CHAMPAGNE

Serves 6

Rose Hill Plantation

Rose Hill Plantation

HERBED TOMATO CONSOMMÉ

2 cups cocktail vegetable juice
2 cups beef broth
1 cup Chablis or other dry white wine
½ cup dry sherry
1 teaspoon dried whole basil leaves
2 whole peppercorns
1 small bay leaf
1 green onion, finely chopped
1 clove garlic, halved
Fresh basil leaves (optional)

Combine all ingredients, except fresh basil leaves, in a large non-aluminum saucepan; bring to a boil, and boil 1 minute. Strain mixture, and discard residue. Serve consommé hot or chilled in mugs; garnish with basil leaves, if desired. Yield: about 5 cups.

Note: Pour consommé into an insulated container to keep hot or chilled for a picnic.

Polo game underway at Rose Hill Plantation. The oldest team sport in the world is relatively new to the South.

COLD ROAST QUAIL WITH SAVORY ORANGE SAUCE

12 quail, dressed
12 slices bacon
1 teaspoon salt
¼ teaspoon pepper
Savory Orange Sauce

Wrap each quail with a slice of bacon; place each on a 12-inch square of aluminum foil. Sprinkle evenly with salt and pepper. Bring corners of foil together; fold edges over loosely to seal.

Place packets on baking sheets. Bake at 325° for 1 hour or until quail is tender. Open foil; broil quail 6 inches from heating element 4 minutes or until browned. Cover and chill thoroughly. Serve cold with Savory Orange Sauce. Yield: 6 servings.

Savory Orange Sauce:

1 (10-ounce) jar orange marmalade
1 tablespoon plus 1½ teaspoons Dijon mustard
½ teaspoon ground ginger

Combine all ingredients in a small mixing bowl, stirring well. Cover and store in refrigerator. Yield: about 1 cup.

Rose Hill Plantation's Gothic Revival style is atypical of Southern architecture.

WALDORF SALAD WITH WINE

4 unpeeled Winesap or Jonathan apples, cored and cut into cubes
1 stalk celery, chopped
1 cup seedless grapes
½ cup chopped walnuts
½ cup mayonnaise
¼ cup dry white wine
6 lettuce cups

Combine apples, celery, grapes, and walnuts in a medium mixing bowl.

Combine mayonnaise and wine, stirring well. Pour over fruit mixture; toss lightly. Cover and refrigerate until chilled. Serve in lettuce cups. Yield: 6 servings.

FRENCH BREAD

6 cups all-purpose flour,
  divided
2 tablespoons sugar
2 teaspoons salt
2 packages dry yeast
2 cups water
¼ cup shortening, melted
1 egg white, beaten

Combine 2 cups flour, sugar, salt, and yeast in large mixing bowl. Set aside.

Combine water and shortening in a small saucepan, and cook until very warm (120° to 130°); add to flour mixture. Blend mixture at low speed of an electric mixer until dry ingredients are moistened. Beat 3 minutes at medium speed. Stir in 3½ cups flour to make a soft dough.

Turn dough out onto a lightly floured surface, and knead 10 minutes or until smooth and elastic, working in ½ cup flour, if needed.

Shape dough into a ball; place in a greased bowl, turning to grease top. Cover and let rise in a warm place (85°), free from drafts, 1 hour or until doubled in bulk.

Punch dough down; divide in half. Cover and let rest 5 minutes. Shape each half into an 18- x 3-inch loaf. Place loaves 4 inches apart on a lightly greased baking sheet.

Cut diagonal slashes, 1½ inches apart and ¼-inch deep, across top of each loaf. Cover and repeat rising procedure 35 minutes or until doubled in bulk. Bake at 425° for 15 minutes; reduce heat to 350°, and bake 25 minutes or until loaves sound hollow when tapped.

Remove baking sheet from oven; brush each loaf lightly with beaten egg white. Return bread to oven 2 minutes. Remove bread from baking sheet immediately; cool on wire racks. Yield: 2 loaves.

Herbed Tomato Consommé (page 31) and French Bread.

HOT SPICED COMPOTE

2 oranges, sliced and seeded
1½ cups water
1 (15½-ounce) can pineapple
  chunks, undrained
1 (16-ounce) can sliced
  peaches, undrained
½ teaspoon grated lemon rind
5 whole cloves
3 (3-inch) sticks cinnamon
¼ teaspoon ground nutmeg
1 (16-ounce) can purple
  plums, drained
1 (11-ounce) can mandarin
  oranges, drained
3 tablespoons Cognac

Cut orange slices in half. Combine orange slices and water in a medium-size non-aluminum saucepan; bring to a boil. Reduce heat; simmer, uncovered, 25 minutes. Strain, discarding pulp.

Drain pineapple and peaches, reserving juice. Combine hot orange liquid, reserved pineapple and peach juice, lemon rind, cloves, cinnamon, and nutmeg in non-aluminum saucepan. Bring to a boil. Reduce heat; simmer, uncovered, 30 minutes. Add pineapple, peaches, plums, and mandarin oranges; heat thoroughly. Stir in Cognac. Serve in dessert bowls. Yield: about 6 cups.

Note: Ladle into an insulated container for a picnic.

XIT ranch hands on a roundup, 1888.

XIT RODEO AND REUNION BARBECUE

Reach for your superlatives, partner; we are going to talk about Texas. In the 1880s, the XIT was the largest range under fence in the world; it covered parts of ten counties in the Texas Panhandle and ran 150,000 head of cattle. The first XIT association was formed in 1936 at the Old Settlers Reunion in Amarillo. In 1937, Dalhart became permanent headquarters, and the first free barbecue was held. Now it is the largest amateur rodeo and free barbecue in the world. Every August, on the first full weekend, more than 25,000 people come to eat corn-on-the-cob the first day, watermelon the next, and on the final day: barbecue, cooked in two 75-foot-long pits.

BARBECUED BEEF
BEER BEANS
SLICED ONION * DILL PICKLE SPEARS
TEXAS TOAST
APPLESAUCE À LA MODE
ICED TEA
BEER

Serves 8

"Round up" the folks for Barbecued Beef and Beer Beans.

BEER BEANS

1 (16-ounce) package dried
  pinto beans
1 (12-ounce) can beer
2 quarts water
3 large ripe tomatoes, peeled,
  seeded, and chopped
2 large onions, chopped
2 cloves garlic, crushed
2 tablespoons chili powder
2 teaspoons garlic salt
2 teaspoons cumin seeds
2 teaspoons salt
1 teaspoon pepper

Place beans in a large sauce-pan. Cover with water 3 inches above beans; let soak overnight.

Drain beans, and return to saucepan; add beer. Slowly bring to a boil. Reduce heat; simmer, uncovered, 30 minutes or until beer has evaporated.

Add remaining ingredients, stirring well. Bring to a boil. Reduce heat; cover and simmer 1 hour. Uncover and continue to simmer 2 hours or until beans are tender. Yield: 2 quarts.

TEXAS TOAST

8 thick slices white bread
Softened butter

Spread butter on both sides of bread. Grill over medium-hot coals until browned, turning once. Yield: 8 servings.

APPLESAUCE
À LA MODE

8 medium cooking apples (2½
  pounds), peeled, cored, and
  quartered
½ cup water
½ cup sugar
1 teaspoon vanilla extract
Vanilla ice cream

Combine apples and water in a large saucepan. Cover and bring to a boil. Reduce heat; simmer 20 minutes or until apples are tender. Mash apples.

Add sugar and vanilla, stirring until sugar dissolves. Serve warm or cold, and top with ice cream. Yield: 5 cups.

BARBECUED BEEF

1 (5- to 6-pound) boneless
  beef brisket
1 teaspoon salt
2 teaspoons pepper
8 mesquite or hickory chips
Basting Sauce

Sprinkle brisket with salt and pepper; set aside 1 hour.

Soak mesquite chips in water to cover; set aside.

Prepare charcoal fire in grill, and let burn 45 minutes to 1 hour or until coals are white and moderately hot. Drain mesquite chips, and add 4 chips to charcoal, reserving remaining chips.

Place brisket on grill 8 inches from coals. Cover and cook over coals 4 to 5 hours or until desired degree of doneness. Turn brisket, and baste with Basting Sauce every 20 minutes. Add charcoal and soaked chips to fire as necessary to maintain heat and smoke.

To serve, cut diagonally across the grain into thin slices. Yield: 8 servings.

Basting Sauce:

1 quart vinegar
1 cup lard
1 large onion, finely chopped
1 medium lemon, thinly
  sliced
1 teaspoon garlic salt

Combine all ingredients in a large saucepan; bring to a boil. Cook over medium heat 5 minutes, stirring occasionally. Yield: about 1½ quarts.

Note: Basting Sauce may be made ahead of time.

FORT WORTH EXPOSITION FARE

Back in 1896, some foresighted cattlemen put on a fat stock show in Fort Worth to attract national meat-packers to Texas. The modest one-day event had the desired effect. The next year, tents were erected, and people paid twenty-five cents to see the stock. Growth was rapid. In 1905, the North Side Coliseum was built to house the show. On the night before it opened, Fort Worth society joined in a kermis and two elegant balls. In 1917, the World's Original Indoor Rodeo was added to the list of entertainments. Chief Quanah Parker's Comanche warriors performed war games. The spectators were also thrilled by the wild bucking horses, especially one named "Five Minutes to Midnight." The show moved to the Will Rogers Coliseum in 1944. Today the exposition involves twenty buildings in Amon Carter Square. What does one eat when the big ten-day show is going on? Steak, naturally!

BROILED RIB EYES
CALF FRIES
CAMP-STYLE POTATOES
TOSSED SALAD WITH GARLIC DRESSING
DEWBERRY COBBLER

Serves 6

BROILED RIB EYES

6 (¾-pound) rib eyes, 1 inch thick
Salt and pepper to taste

Place rib eyes on a well-greased rack in a shallow roasting pan. Broil 5 to 6 inches from heating element 8 to 10 minutes on each side or until desired degree of doneness. Transfer rib eyes to a warm serving platter, and sprinkle with salt and pepper to taste. Serve immediately. Yield: 6 servings.

CALF FRIES

12 calf fries (3 pounds) with sac
1 cup milk
1 egg
1½ cups all-purpose flour
¾ cup cornmeal
1½ teaspoons salt
½ teaspoon pepper
Vegetable oil

Place calf fries with sacs on a baking sheet, and freeze.

Slit each sac; pull away from calf fries, and discard. Slice calf fries into thick strips.

Combine milk and egg in a medium mixing bowl, beating well. Add calf fries, and soak 1 hour. Drain, discarding milk mixture.

Combine flour, cornmeal, salt, and pepper; dredge in flour mixture, and fry in deep, hot oil (375°) until golden brown. Drain well on paper towels. Serve hot. Yield: 6 servings.

Calf Fries and "go-withs": Tossed Salad with Garlic Dressing and Camp-Style Potatoes (page 36).

Chief Quanah Parker and company at Southwestern Exposition and Fat Stock Show, 1920.

CAMP-STYLE POTATOES

½ pound bacon, diced
1 medium onion, chopped
1 medium-size green pepper,
    seeded and chopped
2½ pounds potatoes,
    scrubbed and sliced
1 (10-ounce) can tomatoes
    with chiles
Salt and pepper to taste

Cook bacon in a large skillet until browned. Add onion and green pepper; sauté until tender. Drain off fat, if desired.

Add potatoes and tomatoes, stirring lightly. Reduce heat; cover and simmer 15 minutes or until potatoes are tender. Add salt and pepper to taste. Yield: 6 servings.

TOSSED SALAD WITH GARLIC DRESSING

1 large clove garlic,
    halved
1 head iceberg lettuce
1 head endive lettuce
6 green onion fans
Garlic Dressing

Rub the inside of a large salad bowl with cut sides of garlic; discard garlic, and set bowl aside.

Separate lettuce leaves; wash and drain thoroughly. Tear into bite-size pieces.

Combine lettuce and green onion fans in prepared salad bowl; toss lightly to mix well. Cover and chill thoroughly. Serve salad with Garlic Dressing. Yield: 6 servings.

Garlic Dressing:

4 eggs
1 teaspoon salt
1 teaspoon dry mustard
1 tablespoon vinegar
1 tablespoon lemon juice
1⅔ cups vegetable oil
4 hard-cooked eggs, finely
    chopped
4 cloves garlic, minced
5 sprigs fresh parsley
4 green onions, chopped

Place 4 eggs in container of an electric blender; process 5 seconds. Add salt, mustard, vinegar, and lemon juice; process an additional 5 seconds while adding oil in a thin, steady stream. Add hard-cooked eggs, garlic, parsley, and green onion; blend well. Cover and chill thoroughly. Yield: 3¾ cups.

Breeders with prize stock at Fort Worth show, circa 1920.

DEWBERRY COBBLER

2¼ cups all-purpose flour
1 teaspoon salt
¾ cup shortening
2 eggs, beaten
¼ cup milk
5 cups fresh dewberries or
  blackberries
2 cups sugar
2 tablespoons butter
Vanilla ice cream

Combine flour and salt in a large mixing bowl, stirring well; cut in shortening with a pastry blender until mixture resembles coarse meal. Add eggs and milk; stir with a fork just until dry ingredients are moistened.

Turn out onto a heavily floured surface, and knead 2 or 3 times. Roll one-fourth of pastry on a floured surface into a 10- x 6-inch rectangle, and cut into 10- x 1-inch strips. Place strips on an ungreased baking sheet; bake at 450° for 5 minutes. Let cool on baking sheet.

Divide remaining dough in half. Roll one half to ⅛-inch thickness on a lightly floured surface, and fit into a 10- x 6- x 2-inch baking dish. Set aside prepared dish and remaining portion of dough.

Combine berries and sugar; toss lightly to coat well. Spoon half of berries evenly into prepared dish; carefully arrange baked pastry strips over top. Spoon remaining berries over strips; dot with butter.

Roll remaining dough to ¼-inch thickness on a floured surface. Carefully place over berries. Trim edges; seal and flute. Cut slits in top crust. Bake at 450° for 20 minutes; reduce temperature to 350°, and bake an additional 15 minutes or until golden brown. Serve warm, and top with ice cream. Yield: 6 servings.

Owner shows off fine horses, Fort Worth, circa 1920.

HUNTER'S CHOICE

MENU OF MENUS

ST. JOHN'S HUNTING
CLUB FEAST

RED RIVER VALLEY
HUNTERS' MEAL

HUNTERS' BREAKFAST IN
THOMASVILLE

MAGNOLIA SPRINGS HUNT
FEAST

WOOLAROC GAME FEAST

ARKANSAS
DUCK HUNTERS'
SUPPER

NATIONAL FIELD TRIAL
FISH FRY

TURKEY CALLING
CONTEST DINNER

*Hunters' dream menu:
Platter of Pheasant aux
Fines Herbes (front), Onions
Baked in Wine, chafing
dish filled with Ragout of
Venison, Smoked Duck with
Wild Duck Dressing, and
Cranberry-Orange Relish.*

Perhaps more so than in other parts of the country, the South retains an active interest in game hunting. Nowadays it is deemed a sport rather than a way to stay alive. Hunting even appeals to many of today's women; there are female hunters as adept at field-dressing a deer or as patient while waiting out the ducks from behind a chilly blind as any man in the party.

Such a woman would have been rare, though, in 1904. That was the year the W. B. Sharps came to Houston, where Sharp was active in the Humble Oil (now Exxon) Company. Mrs. Sharp found Houston, then a town of 40,000, "physically primitive but with a strong backing of Southern culture." She related that during hunting season, when dove and quail were plentiful, the men would take over the kitchen, serving meals of birds, biscuits, and coffee. No alcoholic beverages were served. At this point in her story, one wonders what became of the Southern culture in which Houston's society was rooted. How unlike a Southerner not to imbibe in the social context of the hunting season. A hunt might be dismal or successful; toasts at the ensuing party consoled or celebrated.

President William Howard Taft once attended a game breakfast in Savannah at the home of Juliet Gordon Low, founder of the Girl Scouts of America. After warming up with shrimp and hominy, the president downed potted partridge, broiled venison, grilled partridge, and more venison. Then, while his driver waited, Mr. Taft helped himself to some waffles, hot rolls—and more venison. Mrs. Low, who had been summoned from England by her family to assist with the memorable event, was impressed by his girth.

Meals served up with the wild game from the hunt delight the palate of all, not just the hunter's. Any hunter who has contributed to a wild game breakfast or supper will agree that sharing the rewards is the fun of it all. That is why we can enjoy the pleasures of the menus in this chapter.

Other hunt-related events in the South invite the pleasure of the nonhunter. The royalty among hunting dogs compete in the National Field Trial Championship in Grand Junction, Tennessee, and the National Wild Turkey Calling Contest is held every October in Yellville, Arkansas.

ST. JOHN'S HUNTING CLUB FEAST

In 1800, the year the Santee Canal opened, the St. John's Hunting Club was organized in South Carolina. The twelve men of the Black Oak community who met at Woodboo Plantation to form the club rules were the third and fourth generation of original settlers. *Rule Four:* "Each member shall find a dinner, in turn. . . ."

Incredible quantities of food and strong drink were mandated. In 1900, club dinners became semi-annual affairs, paid for by dues, and *hunting* became strictly nominal in the club name. The clubhouse is on part of the old Pooshee Plantation, nearly all that is left of the founders' lands, now flooded by the Santee-Cooper hydroelectric project.

RAGOUT OF VENISON
SMOKED DUCK
WILD DUCK DRESSING
PHEASANT AUX FINES HERBES
WILD RICE AND CHEESE CASSEROLE
ONIONS BAKED IN WINE
CRANBERRY-ORANGE RELISH
CHOCOLATE REFRIGERATOR PIE

Serves 8

RAGOUT OF VENISON

4 slices bacon
1 (3-pound) venison roast, cut into 1-inch cubes
3 large onions, chopped
5 cloves garlic, minced
1 quart water
1 (10¾-ounce) can beef broth, undiluted
½ cup beer
2 tablespoons bourbon
1 teaspoon salt
½ teaspoon curry powder
½ pound fresh mushrooms, sliced
Hot cooked rice

Cook bacon in a large skillet until crisp; remove bacon, reserving drippings. Crumble bacon, and set aside.

Add venison, onion, and garlic to drippings; cook, stirring frequently, until meat is browned. Add water, beef broth, beer, bourbon, salt, and curry powder, stirring well. Cover and simmer 50 minutes, stirring occasionally. Add reserved bacon and sliced mushrooms; cover and simmer an additional 10 minutes. Ladle over rice in individual serving bowls. Yield: 1½ quarts.

SMOKED DUCK

1 (5- to 5½-pound) duck
2 quarts water
¼ teaspoon hot sauce
½ cup Worcestershire sauce
¼ cup commercial meat-curing mixture
2 (25.4-ounce) bottles Burgundy or other dry red wine
Spiced apple rings
Fresh parsley sprigs

Remove giblets and neck from duck; reserve for other uses. Rinse duck thoroughly with cold water, and pat dry. Prick fatty areas, except breast, with a fork. Place duck in a large plastic bag with seal.

Combine water, hot sauce, Worcestershire sauce, and salt; stir well. Pour over duck in plastic bag; seal bag, and refrigerate overnight. Remove duck, discarding liquid. Rinse duck thoroughly with cold water; pat dry. Lift wingtips up and over back, tucking under duck securely. Fold neck skin under.

Prepare fire in smoker, and let burn 10 to 15 minutes. Place water pan in smoker, and fill with 1 bottle of wine. Add enough hot water to fill pan.

Place prepared duck on food rack. Cover with smoker lid; cook 8 hours or until drumsticks are easy to move, refilling water pan with additional wine and water as needed.

Transfer duck to a serving platter; cool 15 minutes before carving. Garnish with apple and parsley. Yield: 8 servings.

A setting familiar to every hunt club in the South: a stately portrait looks on as table is prepared for a wild game dinner.

WILD DUCK DRESSING

Southern Cornbread
4 cups fine dry breadcrumbs
1½ cups finely chopped
   celery
1 cup finely chopped
   onion
⅔ cup finely chopped green
   pepper
¼ cup bacon drippings
1 chicken-flavored bouillon
   cube
1 quart warm water
2 teaspoons rubbed sage
1 teaspoon poultry seasoning
1 tablespoon salt
1 teaspoon pepper
2 eggs, beaten

Combine 4 cups Southern Cornbread crumbs and bread-crumbs in a large bowl; set aside. (Reserve remaining corn-bread for other uses.)

Sauté celery, onion, and green pepper in bacon drippings until tender; add to crumb mixture, stirring well.

Dissolve bouillon cube in warm water. Stir bouillon mix-ture and remaining ingredients into crumb mixture. Spoon into a lightly greased 13- x 9- x 2-inch baking dish. Bake at 350° for 45 minutes or until lightly browned. Yield: 8 servings.

Southern Cornbread:

1 cup all-purpose flour
1 cup yellow cornmeal
1 tablespoon plus 1 teaspoon
   baking powder
¾ teaspoon salt
2 eggs, beaten
1 cup milk
¼ cup vegetable oil

Combine flour, cornmeal, baking powder, and salt in a large mixing bowl; mix well.

Combine eggs, milk, and oil in a small mixing bowl, mixing until well blended. Slowly pour over cornmeal mixture, stirring just until dry ingredients are moistened.

Pour batter into a well-greased 9-inch square pan. Bake at 425° for 20 minutes or until lightly browned. Yield: 6 to 8 servings.

Lifelike pintail drake decoy carved by Ward Brothers, Crisfield, Maryland, 1936.

North American Wildfowl Art Museum

PHEASANT AUX FINES HERBES

3 tablespoons olive oil
3 tablespoons butter or
   margarine
4 (1-pound) pheasant, dressed
   and split
2 medium onions
4 whole cloves
3 cloves garlic, minced
½ pound fresh mushrooms,
   sliced
2½ cups Chablis or other dry
   white wine
¼ cup chopped fresh parsley
2 bay leaves
¼ teaspoon dried whole
   thyme
Hot cooked rice
Purple savoy cabbage

Combine olive oil and butter in a large skillet; cook over me-dium heat until butter melts. Add pheasant, and sauté until lightly browned. Transfer to paper towels to drain; set aside skillet with oil mixture. Cut a ½-inch slice from the bottom of 1 onion; insert cloves, and set aside. Chop remaining onion. Add chopped onion, garlic, and mushrooms to oil mixture in skillet; sauté until tender.

Return pheasant to skillet. Add wine, parsley, bay leaves, thyme, and reserved onion slice. Cover and simmer 30 minutes or until tender. Discard bay leaves and onion slice.

Serve pheasant halves over rice; spoon vegetable mixture over pheasant. Garnish with cabbage. Yield: 8 servings.

WILD RICE AND CHEESE CASSEROLE

1 (4-ounce) package wild rice
½ cup butter or margarine
2 tablespoons all-purpose
   flour
1 cup milk
1 teaspoon salt
1 (3-ounce) package softened
   cream cheese
2 (4-ounce) cans button
   mushrooms, drained

Cook wild rice according to package directions; drain and set aside.

Melt butter in top of a double boiler over simmering water; add flour, stirring until smooth. Cook 1 minute, stirring con-stantly. Gradually add milk; cook over boiling water, stirring constantly, until thickened and bubbly. Stir in salt and cream cheese. Remove from heat.

Grease a 1½-quart casserole. Spoon half of wild rice into dish; place half of mushrooms on top of rice, and spoon half of cream cheese sauce evenly over mush-rooms. Repeat layering proce-dure. Bake at 325° for 30 minutes. Serve hot. Yield: 8 servings.

ONIONS BAKED IN WINE

2 tablespoons butter or margarine
2 tablespoons vegetable oil
20 small onions (about 1½ inches in diameter), peeled
¾ cup Chablis or other dry white wine
3 sprigs fresh parsley
⅛ teaspoon ground thyme
Dash of salt
Dash of pepper
1 small bay leaf

Melt butter in a large skillet over low heat; add oil and onions. Sauté over medium heat 15 minutes or until onions become slightly tender and lightly browned, stirring frequently. Remove from heat, and transfer to a 10- x 6- x 2-inch baking dish. Combine remaining ingredients, stirring well; pour over onions in dish.

Cover with aluminum foil; bake at 350° for 45 minutes or until onions are tender. Remove and discard bay leaf. Serve hot. Yield: 8 servings.

CRANBERRY-ORANGE RELISH

2 cups fresh cranberries
1 large orange, unpeeled, cut into eighths and seeded
½ cup pecans
½ cup sugar
2 tablespoons Grand Marnier or other orange-flavored liqueur
Additional fresh cranberries
Orange sections

Process 2 cups cranberries, orange, and pecans through a food grinder. Combine mixture with sugar and Grand Marnier in a small mixing bowl; cover and chill thoroughly.

To serve, garnish with additional cranberries and orange sections. Yield: 2½ cups.

Label from Hunting Club Whiskey, c.1900. Trained dog retrieves woodcock.

CHOCOLATE REFRIGERATOR PIE

1½ cups sugar
½ cup plus 1 tablespoon all-purpose flour
¼ cup plus 2 teaspoons cocoa
⅛ teaspoon salt
2¼ cups milk, scalded
3 eggs, beaten
1 tablespoon butter or margarine
1½ teaspoons vanilla extract
1 baked (9-inch) pastry shell
Sweetened whipped cream
Chocolate curls

Combine sugar, flour, cocoa, and salt in a large heavy saucepan, stirring to remove lumps. Gradually add scalded milk, stirring until well blended. Cook over medium heat, stirring constantly, until mixture comes to a boil and thickens. Cook an additional minute, stirring constantly to prevent scorching.

Gradually stir one-fourth of hot mixture into beaten eggs; add to remaining hot mixture, stirring constantly. Cook, stirring constantly, 2 minutes or until mixture thickens. Remove from heat; add butter and vanilla, stirring until butter melts. Pour mixture into baked pastry shell; chill thoroughly. To serve, garnish with whipped cream and chocolate curls. Yield: one 9-inch pie.

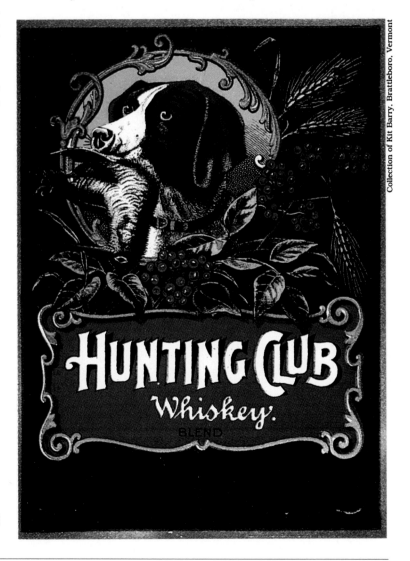

Collection of Kit Barry, Brattleboro, Vermont

RED RIVER VALLEY HUNTERS' MEAL

The Red River, in its middle and lower eastward course along the Oklahoma-Texas boundary, picks up the rich red soil that gives it its name. In the early part of the twentieth century, men and boys went on hunting and fishing trips along the river; they traveled in wagons, in buggies, or on horseback. Slang Jang, the main dish in this menu, came about like this: on a sultry day, a hunting party far north of Honey Grove decided it was too hot to cook. They formulated, on the spot, a hearty dish they named for the cattle bells they could hear in the distance. Apochryphal? Maybe, but Slang Jang has been a favorite at holiday dinners for decades in Oklahoma.

SLANG JANG
LONGHORN CHEESE
DEVIL DOGS
SUGAR COOKIES

Serves 12

SLANG JANG

3 (8-ounce) cans cove oysters, drained and chopped
3 large heads cabbage, chopped
2 (16-ounce) jars sweet pickles, drained and chopped
2 (16-ounce) jars sour pickles, drained and chopped
1 (16-ounce) can tomatoes, drained and chopped
4 large green peppers, seeded and chopped
2 large onions, chopped
2 cooking apples, cored and chopped
1 large stalk celery, chopped
½ pod red pepper, chopped
1 small clove garlic, minced
3 hard-cooked eggs, sliced
Salt and pepper to taste
1½ teaspoons dry mustard
3 pounds Longhorn cheese, sliced
Assorted crackers

Combine first 12 ingredients in a large container; stir well. Add salt, pepper, and mustard; mix well. Serve with Longhorn cheese and assorted crackers. Yield: 12 servings.

Oklahomans like Slang Jang with Longhorn cheese and crackers.

Texas hunting party picnicking near El Campo, Texas, circa 1915.

DEVIL DOGS

½ cup shortening
1 cup sugar
1 egg
2 cups all-purpose flour
½ cup cocoa
1¼ teaspoons baking soda
½ teaspoon baking powder
¼ teaspoon salt
1 cup milk
1 teaspoon vanilla extract
Filling (recipe follows)

Cream shortening in a large mixing bowl; gradually add sugar, beating well. Add egg, beating well.

Combine flour, cocoa, soda, baking powder, and salt; mix well. Add to creamed mixture alternately with milk, beginning and ending with flour mixture; stir well. Stir in vanilla.

Drop mixture by teaspoonfuls onto ungreased cookie sheets. Bake at 375° for 8 minutes. Remove from cookie sheets, and cool completely on wire racks. Spread half of cookies with filling; top with remaining cookies. Yield: 2 dozen.

Filling:

½ cup butter or margarine, softened
1½ cups sifted powdered sugar
¾ cup marshmallow creme
1 teaspoon vanilla extract

Cream butter in a medium mixing bowl until light and fluffy; gradually add sugar, beating well after each addition. Add marshmallow cream and vanilla; beat well. Yield: filling for 2 dozen filled cookies.

SUGAR COOKIES

1 cup butter, softened
1½ cups sifted powdered sugar
1 egg
1 teaspoon vanilla extract
½ teaspoon almond extract
2½ cups all-purpose flour
1 teaspoon cream of tartar
1 teaspoon baking soda
Sugar

Cream butter in a medium

mixing bowl; gradually add powdered sugar, beating until light and fluffy. Add egg, beating well. Stir in flavorings.

Sift together flour, cream of tartar, and soda in a medium mixing bowl. Gradually add to creamed mixture, stirring until well blended. Cover and chill at least 2 hours.

Divide dough in half. Turn half of dough out onto a well-floured surface. (Keep remaining dough chilled until ready to use.) Roll to ⅛-inch thickness; cut with a floured 2½-inch round cutter.

Place cookies 1 inch apart on ungreased cookie sheets. Bake at 375° for 7 minutes or until edges are lightly browned. Remove from cookie sheets; sprinkle tops with sugar, and cool on wire racks. Repeat procedure with remaining dough. Yield: about 5 dozen.

HUNTERS' BREAKFAST IN THOMASVILLE

he railroad from Savannah to Thomasville, in Southwest Georgia, was a lifeline for the Confederacy throughout the Civil War. A temporary internment camp at Thomasville held a contingent of Northern soldiers toward the end of the war, and it was they who sang Thomasville's praises in the North and made the town the first winter resort of the South. The 1880s and 1890s brought wealthy industrialists and financiers by rail from Northern cities to the fresh pine air of Thomasville, a town left undamaged by war. They hunted the plentiful bobwhite quail and wild turkey and fished the warm semitropical waters. How splendid their quail breakfasts were!

BREAKFAST QUAIL
EGGS CHAUSSEUR
HOT BUTTERED GRITS
TOMATO CHUTNEY
DATE-NUT SQUARES
APPLE CASSEROLE
COFFEE

Serves 12

Breakfast Quail, Tomato Chutney, and hot buttered grits.

BREAKFAST QUAIL

Salt and pepper
12 quail, dressed
1½ cups all-purpose flour, divided
Vegetable oil
1 quart milk
½ teaspoon salt
½ teaspoon pepper
1 teaspoon Worcestershire sauce

Sprinkle salt and pepper over quail; dredge in 1 cup flour, coating well. Heat ¼ inch oil in a large skillet; add quail, and fry over medium heat 10 minutes or until golden brown, turning occasionally. Drain.

Pour off drippings, reserving ½ cup in skillet. Add remaining ½ cup flour to reserved drippings; cook over low heat 1 minute, stirring until smooth. Gradually add milk; cook over medium heat, stirring constantly, until thickened and bubbly. Stir in ½ teaspoon salt, ½ teaspoon pepper, and Worcestershire sauce.

Return quail to skillet with gravy; cover and simmer 1 hour. Arrange quail on a serving platter. Serve immediately with gravy. Yield: 12 servings.

EGGS CHAUSSEUR

½ cup butter or margarine,
   divided
1 pound chicken livers
1 cup sliced mushrooms
White Sauce
16 eggs
⅔ cup whipping cream
½ teaspoon salt
¼ teaspoon pepper
Fresh parsley sprigs

Melt ¼ cup butter in a large
skillet; add livers and mushrooms. Cook over medium heat,
stirring occasionally, 30 minutes or until liquid is absorbed.

Add liver mixture to White
Sauce; stir well. Spoon into center of a warm serving platter;
keep warm.

Combine eggs, whipping
cream, salt, and pepper; beat
well with a wire whisk.

Melt remaining butter in a
large skillet over medium heat;
add egg mixture. Cook over medium heat, stirring occasionally, until eggs are set. Spoon
eggs around liver mixture on
serving platter; garnish with
parsley. Serve immediately.
Yield: 12 servings.

White Sauce:

1 tablespoon plus 1½
   teaspoons butter or
   margarine
3 tablespoons all-purpose
   flour
1½ cups milk
¾ teaspoon salt
¼ teaspoon white pepper

Melt butter in a heavy saucepan over low heat; add flour,
stirring with a wire whisk until
smooth. Cook 1 minute, stirring constantly. Gradually add
milk; cook over medium heat,
stirring constantly, until thickened and bubbly. Stir in salt
and pepper. Yield: 1½ cups.

*American Field Sports/
On a Point is the title of
this color lithograph
by Currier and Ives, 1857.*

That pine-scented air
had a healing effect on
the lungs was a pre-
vailing belief in the 1880s.
Thomasville had more than
enough to share with
wealthy Northerners, who
further appreciated being
able to hunt in the game-rich
forests during mild winters.
Although it had given its
share of men to the Civil
War, residents harbored less
rancor than, say, Atlanta;
physically, at least, Thomasville had been unscathed.

A hunting camp near Frederick, Maryland, circa 1900.

TOMATO CHUTNEY

1 (28-ounce) can whole
  tomatoes, undrained and
  chopped
1¼ cups sugar
1¼ cups red wine vinegar
1 clove garlic, minced
¼ cup golden raisins

Combine tomatoes and sugar in a medium saucepan, stirring well; bring to a boil. Add wine vinegar and minced garlic, stirring well; return to a boil. Reduce heat, and cook, stirring frequently, 1½ to 2 hours or until mixture thickens and reaches consistency of jelly. Add raisins, and cook 5 minutes, stirring frequently to prevent scorching. Yield: 2 cups.

DATE-NUT SQUARES

36 saltine crackers, crushed
2½ cups sugar
1½ teaspoons baking powder
1 (8-ounce) package pitted
  dates, finely chopped
1½ cups chopped pecans
9 egg whites
¼ teaspoon almond extract

Combine cracker crumbs, sugar, and baking powder in a large mixing bowl; add dates and pecans, mixing well.

Beat egg whites (at room temperature) in a large mixing bowl until foamy; add almond extract, and continue beating until stiff peaks form. Fold into cracker mixture.

Spoon mixture into a greased 13- x 9- x 2-inch baking pan. Bake at 325° for 45 minutes or until a wooden pick inserted in center comes out clean. Cool. Cut into 1½-inch squares. Yield: about 4 dozen.

Ready for the hunt, c.1898.

Institute of Texan Cultures

APPLE CASSEROLE

9 medium-size cooking
  apples, peeled, cored, and
  sliced
1¾ cups plus 1 tablespoon
  firmly packed brown sugar,
  divided
½ cup plus 1 tablespoon
  butter or margarine, divided
2 lemons, thinly sliced
1½ teaspoons ground
  cinnamon
6 slices white bread, crust
  removed
⅓ cup butter or margarine,
  melted
Apple rose (optional)

Combine apples and 1½ cups brown sugar in a large mixing bowl. Arrange a layer of sugared apples in a 13- x 9- x 2-inch baking dish; dot with 3 tablespoons butter. Cut lemon slices in half. Arrange half of slices over apple mixture. Repeat layers, ending with apples. Dot with remaining butter. Sprinkle cinnamon over top. Bake at 350° for 35 minutes or until apples are tender.

Cut each bread slice into 4 triangles. Dip triangles in melted butter. Arrange on top of casserole; sprinkle remaining brown sugar over top. Broil until triangles are lightly toasted. Let stand 10 minutes. Garnish with apple rose, if desired. Yield: 12 servings.

MAGNOLIA SPRINGS HUNT FEAST

round Magnolia Springs, the land along Mobile Bay in Alabama is alive with game, ripe for the hunting. And the men who work there, on land or on sea, have grown up with a rich heritage of harvesting that game, as well as the fish in the surrounding waters. Sometimes young people move away and return later, bringing their families back for periodic reunions. They fully expect to be greeted with a series of game suppers, barbecues, and parties. And they can always look forward to putting the dogs to work on a quail or dove hunt. Or the game may be rabbit, squirrel, raccoon, opossum, or even nutria. Whatever isn't in season is in the freezer!

PLANTATION DOVE
LEMON-BAKED QUAIL
FRIED RABBIT
SQUIRREL STEW
CONFETTI RICE
PARMESAN SCALLOPED TOMATOES
BRAN BISCUITS
GARLIC BREAD

Serves 8

The Hunters, *an oil on canvas by Gari Melchers, circa 1922.*

Fried Rabbit (front), Bran Biscuits, Squirrel Stew: part of the wild game feast.

PLANTATION DOVE

20 whole dove breasts, boned, skinned, and split
½ cup olive oil
1 teaspoon dry mustard
½ teaspoon curry powder
¼ teaspoon celery salt
¼ teaspoon garlic salt
¼ teaspoon onion salt
1 cup water
Juice of 1 orange
Juice of 1 lemon
1 teaspoon Worcestershire sauce

Dip each breast half in olive oil; place in a shallow roasting pan. Sprinkle evenly with mustard, curry powder, celery salt, garlic salt, and onion salt. Add water to pan. Cover with aluminum foil, and bake at 275° for 30 minutes; uncover and add remaining ingredients to pan. Bake an additional 30 minutes or until dove is tender. Serve hot or cold on a wooden pick. Yield: 8 appetizer servings.

LEMON-BAKED QUAIL

16 quail, dressed
½ cup water
¾ cup lemon juice
½ cup Worcestershire sauce
½ cup olive oil
¼ cup butter or margarine
1 clove garlic, crushed
1 sprig fresh mint, chopped

Place quail in a shallow roasting pan; add water. Cover and bake at 300° for 30 minutes.

Combine remaining ingredients in a medium saucepan; cook over low heat, stirring constantly, until mixture comes to a boil. Pour mixture over quail. Cover and bake an additional hour or until quail is tender, basting often.

Remove cover from roasting pan. Broil quail 4 inches from heating element 3 minutes or until lightly browned. Yield: 8 servings.

FRIED RABBIT

1¼ cups all-purpose flour, divided
1 tablespoon plus 1½ teaspoons salt, divided
¼ teaspoon paprika
¼ teaspoon red pepper
2 (2½-pound) young American rabbits, dressed and quartered
1 cup bacon drippings
2 cups milk
¼ teaspoon pepper
Fresh parsley sprigs

Combine 1 cup flour, 1 tablespoon plus 1 teaspoon salt, paprika, and red pepper, mixing well; dredge rabbit in flour mixture, coating well.

Heat bacon drippings in a large skillet; add rabbit, and brown quickly on all sides. Reduce heat; cook, uncovered, 40 to 45 minutes or until rabbit is tender and golden brown, turning occasionally. Drain well.

Pour off drippings, reserving ¼ cup drippings in skillet. Add remaining ¼ cup flour; stir until smooth. Cook over low heat 2 minutes, stirring constantly. Add milk; cook over medium heat, stirring constantly, 1 minute or until thickened and bubbly. Stir in remaining salt and pepper. Serve gravy with rabbit. Garnish with parsley. Yield: 8 servings.

SQUIRREL STEW

4 squirrels, dressed
1 tablespoon lard
½ cup chopped onion
2 large tomatoes, peeled,
  quartered, and seeded
3 cups fresh lima beans
3 cups fresh corn kernels
2 quarts water
1 tablespoon Worcestershire
  sauce
1 teaspoon salt
½ teaspoon pepper
Dash of red pepper
1 tablespoon plus 1 teaspoon
  all-purpose flour

Cut each squirrel into 8 pieces. Brown squirrel in lard in a stockpot until lightly browned. Remove from stockpot; drain well on paper towels. Add onion to stockpot; sauté until tender. Add squirrel, tomatoes, lima beans, corn, water, Worcestershire sauce, salt, and pepper; stir well. Cover and bring to a boil.

Add a small amount of hot liquid to flour, stirring to make a paste. Add to stew in stockpot, stirring until blended. Reduce heat; cover and simmer 1 hour or until squirrel is tender. Yield: about 1 gallon.

CONFETTI RICE

1½ cups chicken broth
1½ cups uncooked regular
  rice
¾ cup grated carrot
¾ cup chopped celery
¾ cup chopped fresh
  parsley
¾ cup slivered almonds,
  toasted
½ cup chopped green onion

Bring chicken broth to a boil in a medium saucepan; add rice. Reduce heat; cover and simmer 20 minutes or until rice is tender and chicken broth is absorbed. Chill thoroughly.

Combine remaining ingredients, and mix until well blended. Chill thoroughly.

To serve, combine rice and vegetable mixture; toss gently. Serve chilled. Yield: 8 servings.

Trade card for Syracuse Plow Company, c.1890, shows hunting scene.

PARMESAN SCALLOPED TOMATOES

1 medium onion, chopped
2 tablespoons butter or
  margarine
3 (16-ounce) cans Italian-style
  tomatoes, undrained and
  coarsely chopped
1½ teaspoons salt
1 cup seasoned breadcrumbs,
  divided
2 cups (8 ounces) shredded
  sharp Cheddar cheese,
  divided
⅓ cup grated Parmesan
  cheese

Sauté onion in butter in a medium saucepan. Remove from heat; stir in tomatoes and salt.

Pour one-third of tomato mixture into a 12- x 8- x 2-inch baking dish. Sprinkle ⅓ cup breadcrumbs over tomato mixture; sprinkle 1 cup Cheddar cheese over breadcrumbs. Repeat layers, ending with tomato mixture topped with ⅓ cup breadcrumbs.

Bake at 350° for 25 minutes. Sprinkle Parmesan cheese over top; bake an additional 10 minutes or until hot and bubbly. Yield: 8 servings.

BRAN BISCUITS

½ cup milk
1 cup shreds of wheat
  bran cereal
¾ cup all-purpose flour
2½ teaspoons baking powder
½ teaspoon salt
¼ cup shortening
Butter

Combine milk and cereal; set aside.

Combine flour, baking powder, and salt in a large mixing bowl; mix well. Cut in shortening with a pastry blender until mixture resembles coarse meal. Add reserved cereal mixture, stirring with a fork until dry ingredients are moistened.

Turn dough out onto a floured surface; shape into a ball.

Roll dough to ½-inch thickness; cut with a 1¾-inch biscuit cutter. Place biscuits on a greased baking sheet. Bake at 400° for 12 minutes or until biscuits are lightly browned. Serve warm with butter. Yield: about 1 dozen.

GARLIC BREAD

½ cup butter or margarine,
  softened
⅓ cup grated Parmesan
  cheese
2 cloves garlic, crushed
1 (16-ounce) loaf French
  bread, sliced lengthwise

Combine butter, cheese, and garlic; blend well. Spread butter mixture on cut sides of bread. Wrap in aluminum foil; bake at 350° for 15 minutes. Serve warm. Yield: 8 servings.

WOOLAROC GAME FEAST

"There is no such thing as tough buffalo meat," say those who cook it at Woolaroc Lodge near Bartlesville, Oklahoma. "It tastes like beef, only better." Woolaroc (WOOds-LAkes-ROCks), a 3,500-acre wildlife refuge that features a lodge and museum, is the brainchild of Frank Phillips, the late petroleum tycoon. He fell in love with the Osage Hills Country when he made his milestone oil strike there. He put up miles of fence around his property and built a lodge to entertain his friends and, later, the public. Woolaroc opened in 1926 with a beef and buffalo barbecue. There, for twenty years, Phillips entertained the Who's Who of the arts, politics, and business.

BUFFALO ROAST
or
BARBECUED VENISON STEAKS
GRILLED CHICKEN
GREEN BEANS AMANDINE
CHEESE POTATOES
GREEN SALAD WITH FRENCH DRESSING
FRIED APPLE SLICES
CORN PONE
STRAWBERRY SAUCE OVER VANILLA ICE CREAM

Serves 6 to 8

BUFFALO ROAST

1 (7-pound) buffalo chuck roast
3 tablespoons vegetable oil
2 cups water
¼ cup vinegar
2 tablespoons sugar
1 tablespoon salt
¾ teaspoon liquid smoke
1 medium onion, quartered
1 stalk celery, cut into pieces
Easy Barbecue Sauce

Brown buffalo roast on all sides in hot oil in a large oven-proof Dutch oven.

Combine water, vinegar, sugar, salt, and liquid smoke; pour over buffalo roast. Insert meat thermometer. Top with onion and celery.

Cover and bake at 275° until desired degree of doneness: about 1½ hours or 140° (rare); about 2 hours or 160° (medium). Let roast stand 20 minutes before slicing. Transfer to a serving platter, and serve with Easy Barbecue Sauce. Yield: 6 to 8 servings.

Easy Barbecue Sauce:

1 (32-ounce) bottle catsup
½ cup firmly packed brown sugar
½ cup water
½ cup vinegar
¼ cup sugar
¼ cup prepared mustard
2 tablespoons shortening, melted
2 tablespoons Worcestershire sauce
1½ teaspoons salt
1½ teaspoons hot sauce
¾ teaspoon liquid smoke

Combine all ingredients in a small mixing bowl; mix well. Cover and store in refrigerator until ready to use. Yield: about 1½ quarts.

BARBECUED VENISON STEAKS

½ cup butter or margarine
1 (14-ounce) bottle catsup
½ cup vegetable oil
½ cup Worcestershire sauce
⅓ cup red wine vinegar
1 stalk celery, chopped
1 small onion, chopped
1 clove garlic, minced
Juice of 1 lemon
¼ teaspoon salt
⅛ teaspoon pepper
⅛ teaspoon hot sauce
2 pounds venison loin steaks, about ¼ inch thick
Fresh parsley sprigs

Melt butter in a medium saucepan; add remaining ingredients, except steak and parsley, and bring to a boil. Reduce heat; simmer, uncovered, 20 minutes. Remove from heat.

Grill steaks on each side over medium-low coals 5 minutes or until desired degree of doneness, basting with reserved barbecue sauce. Garnish with parsley. Yield: 6 to 8 servings.

Woolaroc menu features Buffalo Roast (rear) and Barbecued Venison Steaks (fron

rank Phillips (left), after fencing his acreage at Woolaroc, purchased five hundred wild and domestic animals. In 1926, he transported ninety buffalo from Fort Pierre, South Dakota, by train. Woolaroc Lodge (below) opened in April of that year with a beef/buffalo barbecue, a Woolaroc tradition for the next twenty-four years of Phillips' life.

GRILLED CHICKEN

8 chicken breast halves, skinned
2 cups soy sauce
1 cup vegetable oil
½ cup vinegar
¼ cup firmly packed brown sugar
1 tablespoon dried whole oregano
1 tablespoon dried whole thyme
2 teaspoons dry mustard

Place chicken in a large Dutch oven with water to cover; bring to a boil. Reduce heat; cover and simmer 15 minutes. Drain.

Combine remaining ingredients, mixing well. Pour over chicken; cover and refrigerate 4 hours, basting frequently. Remove chicken from marinade; drain well.

Grill chicken over medium coals 10 minutes, turning once. Yield: 6 to 8 servings.

GREEN BEANS AMANDINE

12 slices bacon
¾ cup chopped onion
3 (16-ounce) cans French-style green beans, drained
½ cup vinegar
½ teaspoon salt
½ teaspoon pepper
¼ cup plus 1 tablespoon slivered almonds, toasted

Cook bacon in a large skillet until crisp; remove bacon, reserving ¼ cup drippings in skillet. Crumble bacon, and set aside.

Sauté onion in drippings until tender. Add beans, vinegar, salt, and pepper. Cook over medium heat until thoroughly heated. Remove from heat. Cover and refrigerate at least 3 hours.

Combine bean mixture, almonds, and crumbled bacon in a large saucepan. Cook over medium heat until thoroughly heated. Transfer to a serving bowl. Yield: 6 to 8 servings.

CHEESE POTATOES

8 medium potatoes, cleaned
½ pound fresh mushrooms
3 tablespoons butter or margarine
¼ cup plus 2 tablespoons all-purpose flour
3 cups milk
2 cups (8 ounces) shredded Cheddar cheese, divided
¾ cup grated Parmesan cheese
1½ teaspoons salt
¾ teaspoon white pepper
¼ teaspoon red pepper
½ teaspoon ground thyme
½ cup fine dry breadcrumbs

Cook potatoes in boiling salted water to cover 35 minutes or until tender. Drain well; cool slightly. Peel and cut into ½-inch-thick slices; set aside.

Sauté mushrooms in butter in a medium saucepan until tender. Remove mushrooms with a slotted spoon, and set aside. Reserve butter in pan.

Add flour to melted butter in saucepan, stirring until smooth. Cook 1 minute, stirring constantly. Gradually add milk; cook over medium heat, stirring constantly, until mixture is thickened and bubbly. Stir in reserved mushrooms, 1 cup Cheddar cheese, Parmesan cheese, salt, pepper, and thyme.

Place potatoes in a lightly greased 10- x 6- x 2-inch baking dish. Spoon cheese mixture over potatoes. Sprinkle with remaining cheese and breadcrumbs. Bake, uncovered, at 350° for 30 minutes or until lightly browned. Serve warm. Yield: 6 to 8 servings.

GREEN SALAD WITH FRENCH DRESSING

1 cup croutons
3 tablespoons vegetable oil
2 tablespoons grated Parmesan cheese
½ pound fresh spinach, torn into bite-size pieces
2 medium heads Boston lettuce, torn into bite-size pieces
½ pound fresh mushrooms, sliced
6 hard-cooked eggs, cut into wedges
6 slices bacon, cooked, drained, and crumbled
2 teaspoons sesame seeds
French Dressing

Combine croutons and oil; mix well. Sprinkle Parmesan cheese over croutons; set aside.

Combine remaining ingredients, except French Dressing, in a large salad bowl, tossing well to coat. Sprinkle prepared croutons over top. Serve with French Dressing. Yield: 6 to 8 servings.

French Dressing:

1 cup vegetable oil
1 cup catsup
2 tablespoons vinegar
1 tablespoon lemon juice
½ cup sugar
1½ teaspoons onion salt
1½ teaspoons garlic salt
1½ teaspoons celery salt

Combine all ingredients in a small mixing bowl; mix well. Cover and chill. Yield: 2½ cups.

Home demonstrators making ice cream in Roanoke County, Virginia, in 1931. A special occasion treat.

FRIED APPLE SLICES

¼ cup butter
7 medium-size cooking apples, cored and cut into ½-inch-thick rings
2 cups sugar, divided
Ground cinnamon

Melt butter in a large cast-iron skillet. Add half of apple rings; sprinkle with 1 cup sugar. Cover and cook over medium heat 10 minutes or until tender. Transfer apple rings to a warm serving platter, and sprinkle lightly with cinnamon. Repeat procedure with remaining apple rings and sugar. Serve warm. Yield: 6 to 8 servings.

CORN PONE

2 cups cornmeal
1 teaspoon baking powder
½ teaspoon salt
1 tablespoon shortening
1½ cups milk

Combine cornmeal, baking powder, and salt in a medium mixing bowl, stirring well. Cut in shortening with a pastry blender until mixture resembles coarse meal. Add milk, stirring just until dry ingredients are moistened.

Drop batter by tablespoonfuls onto a hot, lightly greased griddle or skillet. Cook until golden brown, turning once. Serve hot. Yield: about 2 dozen.

STRAWBERRY SAUCE OVER VANILLA ICE CREAM

½ cup sugar
2 tablespoons cornstarch
⅔ cup cold water
2 cups sliced fresh strawberries, divided
1 tablespoon butter or margarine
Vanilla ice cream

Combine sugar and cornstarch in a small saucepan; gradually add water, stirring well. Add ½ cup strawberries. Cook over low heat, stirring constantly, until mixture comes to a boil. Simmer 2 minutes. Remove from heat; add butter, stirring until butter melts. Stir in remaining strawberries. Cover and chill thoroughly. Serve over vanilla ice cream. Yield: 2 cups.

ARKANSAS DUCK HUNTERS' SUPPER

Come November, the serious duck hunter will holler up his retriever and make for Stuttgart, Arkansas, known as "The Duck Capital" of the world. Even before the turn of the century, when rice cropping became an added lure to the migratory flyway that passed over eastern Arkansas, ducks knew the Stuttgart area as a wintering habitat. Industrialization has cut into the sport; efficient harvest machines leave less for the ducks to feed on. But even with fewer mallard, Stuttgart retains its title. In 1936, the World's Championship Duck Calling Contest was added to the annual Rice Festival, where one eats Duck Gumbo, of course.

DUCK GUMBO
HOT COOKED RICE
FRENCH BREAD
CHERRY SQUARES

Serves 18

Hunter's Paradise, *a painting by folk artist Tina Mason, 1950.*

DUCK GUMBO

2½ teaspoons salt, divided
1 teaspoon pepper
4 (3½- to 4-pound) ducklings,
   dressed, cut up, and
   skinned
1 cup butter or margarine,
   melted
1½ cups all-purpose flour
4 medium onions, chopped
1 small green pepper, seeded
   and chopped
3 cloves garlic, minced
1 gallon water
2 pounds smoked sausage,
   cut into ½-inch pieces
½ teaspoon red pepper
⅓ cup chopped green onion
   tops
⅓ cup chopped fresh parsley
Hot cooked rice

Sprinkle 1½ teaspoons salt and 1 teaspoon pepper over ducklings; set aside.

Combine melted butter and flour in a large stockpot; cook over medium heat, stirring constantly, 45 minutes or until roux is color of a copper penny. Add onion, green pepper, and minced garlic; continue cooking 15 minutes or until vegetables are tender.

Gradually add water, stirring until well blended. Add reserved duckling, sausage, and red pepper. Simmer, uncovered, 2 hours or until meat begins to fall off bones. Remove from heat; cool slightly. Cover; refrigerate overnight.

Lift off and discard solidified fat from surface. Remove duckling; remove meat from bones, discarding bones. Chop meat into bite-size pieces; return to gumbo.

Add remaining salt, onion, and parsley. Cook over low heat until thoroughly heated. Ladle over hot cooked rice in individual serving bowls. Yield: about 5 quarts.

Duck Gumbo over rice comes after a successful duck hunt. Unsuccessful? Long Island ducklings will do nicely.

FRENCH BREAD

1 package dry yeast
1 cup warm water (105° to
   115°)
1 tablespoon sugar
2 tablespoons shortening
2 teaspoons salt
3 to 3½ cups all-purpose flour
Cornmeal

Combine yeast, water, and sugar in a large mixing bowl, stirring until yeast and sugar dissolve. Let stand 5 minutes or until bubbly. Stir in shortening and salt. Add flour, 1 cup at a time, stirring to form a stiff dough.

Turn dough out onto a floured surface; knead 10 minutes or until smooth and elastic. Place dough in a greased bowl, turning to grease top. Cover and let rise in a warm place (85°), free from drafts, 1½ hours or until doubled in bulk. Turn dough out onto a lightly floured surface; knead 10 minutes.

Divide dough in half; shape each half into a long, thin loaf. Place loaves in well-greased baguette pans that have been sprinkled with cornmeal. Cut 3 or 4 diagonal slashes, ¾-inch deep, in top of each loaf. Brush loaves with water. Leave uncovered, and repeat rising procedure, 1 hour or until doubled in bulk. Brush risen loaves with water.

Place a shallow pan of water on bottom oven rack. Bake loaves at 400° for 15 minutes. Reduce heat to 375°; continue baking 25 minutes or until loaves sound hollow when tapped. Remove bread from pans immediately; cool on wire racks. Yield: 2 loaves.

CHERRY SQUARES

3½ cups sugar, divided
2 eggs, well beaten
¼ cup butter or margarine,
   melted and divided
2 (16-ounce) cans pitted dark
   sweet cherries, undrained
2 cups all-purpose flour
½ teaspoon baking
   soda
¾ teaspoon salt, divided
2 teaspoons ground
   cinnamon
2¼ teaspoons almond extract,
   divided
1 cup chopped pecans
2 tablespoons cornstarch
1 cup whipping cream,
   whipped

Gradually add 2½ cups sugar to beaten eggs in a large mixing bowl, beating well. Stir in 2 tablespoons melted butter. Drain cherries, reserving liquid. Fold cherries into egg mixture.

Combine flour, soda, ½ teaspoon salt, and cinnamon in a medium mixing bowl. Gently fold into egg mixture. Stir in 2 teaspoons almond extract.

Pour batter evenly into a greased and floured 13- x 9- x 2-inch baking pan. Sprinkle pecans evenly over top of batter. Bake at 350° for 1 hour. Cool.

Combine remaining sugar, cornstarch, and remaining salt in a medium saucepan. Stir in reserved cherry juice, remaining butter, and remaining almond extract. Cook over medium heat, stirring constantly, until thickened. Cool.

To serve, cut into 2-inch squares. Place on individual serving plates; spoon sauce over tops, and dollop with whipped cream. Yield: about 2 dozen.

NATIONAL FIELD TRIAL FISH FRY

About thirty-five bird dogs are selected for the most prestigious hunting dog competition in the world, held annually at the Ames Plantation in Grand Junction, Tennessee. Judges look for a dog that uses its nose, eyes, and brain to find singles or coveys. It must possess speed, courage, and stamina. The first National Field Trial Championship was run in West Point, Mississippi, in 1897. The event was moved to Grand Junction, Tennessee, in 1900, about the time Hobart C. Ames, president of the Field Trial Association for forty-five years, purchased an 1847 manor house to serve as its permanent home. A fish fry is held after the competition.

FRIED CATFISH
HUSH PUPPIES
COLESLAW
FRENCH-FRIED POTATOES

Serves 12

Hunting dogs at work; a field trial in Pinehurst, North Carolina, circa 1920.

Fried Catfish, French-Fried Potatoes, Coleslaw, and Hush Puppies make an irresistibly hearty meal.

FRIED CATFISH

12 dressed catfish (about 8
  pounds)
2 teaspoons salt
½ teaspoon paprika
4 cups cornmeal
Vegetable oil
Lemon wedges
Fresh parsley sprigs

Rinse fish thoroughly in cold water, and pat dry.

Sprinkle salt and paprika over fish. Place cornmeal in a plastic bag; add fish, one at a time, and shake until well coated.

Carefully drop fish into deep hot oil (375°). Fry until fish float to the top and are golden brown; drain well on paper towels.

Transfer fish to a warm serving platter; garnish with lemon wedges and parsley. Yield: 12 servings.

HUSH PUPPIES

2 cups cornmeal
1½ cups all-purpose flour
2 teaspoons baking
  powder
1 teaspoon salt
¾ teaspoon sugar
¼ teaspoon red pepper
Dash of garlic powder
1 small bunch green onions,
  chopped
1¾ cups milk
¼ cup vegetable oil
3 eggs, well beaten
Vegetable oil

Combine cornmeal, flour, baking powder, salt, sugar, pepper, garlic powder, and onion in a large mixing bowl. Add milk, ¼ cup oil, and eggs; stirring until well blended.

Carefully drop batter by tablespoonfuls into deep, hot oil (350°), cooking only a few at a time. Fry 3 minutes or until golden brown. Drain well on paper towels. Serve immediately. Yield: about 4 dozen.

COLESLAW

1 medium cabbage, shredded
2 medium onions, finely
  chopped
2 carrots, scraped and
  shredded
1 medium-size green pepper,
  seeded and chopped
¾ cup sugar
¾ cup vegetable oil
¾ cup vinegar
1 teaspoon salt
1 teaspoon dry mustard
1 teaspoon celery seeds
Lettuce cups

Combine first 4 ingredients in a large bowl; toss lightly. Combine sugar, oil, vinegar, salt, mustard, and celery seeds in a small saucepan. Cook until sugar dissolves. Pour over vegetables; stir. Cover and chill. Serve in lettuce cups. Yield: 2 quarts.

FRENCH-FRIED POTATOES

12 medium potatoes,
  peeled
Vegetable oil
Salt and pepper to taste

Cut potatoes into ½-inch-wide slices; cut each slice into ½-inch-thick strips. Drop, one batch at a time, into deep, hot oil (360°). Fry 5 minutes or until golden brown. Drain on paper towels, and sprinkle with salt and pepper to taste. Serve hot. Yield: 12 servings.

TURKEY CALLING CONTEST DINNER

T he Turkey Trot Festival in Yellville, Arkansas, rolls around the second weekend in October getting under way at noon on Friday with a band concert. It is a full program which includes a beauty pageant and a turkey-and-trimmings dinner. But the main event takes place at 2:00 p.m. on Saturday—the National Wild Turkey Calling Contest. The winner must be the best in five categories: Mating Call, Lost Call (old hen in the spring), Cluck (assembly), Lost Kee-Kee of the Young Bird in the Fall, and Early Morning Fly-Down Cackle. A caller has to be quite versatile to take home one of the cash prizes. The National Champion receives a trophy to keep for the year.

SMOKED WILD TURKEY
ROASTED WILD TURKEY BREAST WITH
CREAM GRAVY
MUSHROOM CORNBREAD DRESSING
MASHED POTATOES
SWEET-AND-SOUR CARROTS
FIRE AND ICE SALAD
CLOVERLEAF ROLLS
PUMPKIN CHIFFON PIE

Serves 8

SMOKED WILD TURKEY

1 (12- to 14-pound) wild turkey, dressed
3 quarts cool water
2 cups firmly packed brown sugar
1½ cups salt
3 cloves garlic, peeled and split
2 teaspoons whole black pepper
4 bay leaves

Rinse turkey thoroughly. Combine remaining ingredients in a large stainless steel, enamel, or plastic container, stirring until sugar and salt dissolve. Add turkey to brine solution; cover and let stand at room temperature 2 hours, turning every 30 minutes.

Remove turkey from brine solution; rinse thoroughly with cold water. Set on wire rack over a shallow pan, and let dry. Tie ends of legs with string. Lift wingtips up and over bird, tucking under bird.

Prepare fire in smoker, using 10 to 12 pounds of charcoal. Add 2 to 4 hickory chips that have been soaked in water.

Place water pan in smoker; fill with warm water. Place turkey on food rack; cover with smoker lid. Cook 6 to 8 hours or until drumsticks move easily, refilling water pan, if necessary. Cover and chill thoroughly. Carve into thin slices. Yield: 10 to 12 servings.

ROASTED WILD TURKEY BREAST WITH CREAM GRAVY

1 teaspoon salt
½ teaspoon pepper
2 teaspoons poultry seasoning
1 (8- to 10-pound) wild turkey breast
Vegetable oil
Cream Gravy
Watercress
Fresh mushrooms

Sprinkle seasonings over turkey. Brush entire turkey breast with oil; place on a rack in a roasting pan.

Insert meat thermometer in breast (do not touch bone). Bake at 325° for 2½ hours or until thermometer registers

185°; baste with pan drippings.

Transfer turkey to a serving platter, reserving ½ cup pan drippings for Cream Gravy; let stand 15 minutes before carving. Serve with Cream Gravy. Garnish with watercress and mushrooms. Yield: 8 servings.

Cream Gravy:

½ cup drippings from Roasted Wild Turkey Breast
¼ cup all-purpose flour
3 cups milk
½ teaspoon salt
¼ teaspoon pepper

Combine drippings and flour in a large skillet, stirring until smooth. Cook 1 minute, stirring constantly. Gradually add milk; cook over medium heat, stirring constantly, until thickened and bubbly. Stir in salt and pepper. Yield: about 3 cups.

Roasted Wild Turkey Breast (left); Smoked Wild Turkey with Fire and Ice Salad (page 65). Background: painting for Wild Turkey Bourbon label.

MUSHROOM CORNBREAD DRESSING

1 pound fresh mushrooms,
  coarsely chopped
¼ pound chicken giblets,
  chopped
1½ cups chopped celery
½ cup chopped onion
⅓ cup chopped fresh parsley
¼ cup butter or margarine
6 cups cornbread crumbs
1½ teaspoons dried whole
  basil
¾ teaspoon salt
¾ teaspoon paprika
¼ teaspoon ground nutmeg
2 cups chicken broth

Sauté mushrooms, giblets, celery, onion, and parsley in butter in a large skillet until vegetables are tender and giblets are lightly browned.

Combine cornbread crumbs, basil, salt, paprika, and nutmeg in a large mixing bowl; stir well. Add chicken broth and sautéed mixture, stirring well.

Spoon dressing into a lightly greased 12- x 8- x 2-inch baking dish. Bake, uncovered, at 325° for 30 minutes or until thoroughly heated. Serve immediately. Yield: 8 servings.

Note: Recipe may be doubled, if necessary, to serve more people.

MASHED POTATOES

9 medium potatoes, cleaned
  and peeled
¾ cup milk
¼ cup plus 2 tablespoons
  butter or margarine
1 teaspoon salt
Paprika
Cream Gravy (page 62)

Cut potatoes into quarters. Combine potatoes and boiling water to cover in a large Dutch oven. Cover and cook over medium heat 20 minutes or until tender.

Drain potatoes, and return to Dutch oven. Cook over low heat, stirring constantly, until potatoes are dry. Remove from heat; set aside.

Combine milk and butter in a small saucepan. Cook over medium heat, stirring constantly, until butter melts.

Mash potatoes until smooth. Gradually add milk mixture; stir well. Stir in salt.

Transfer potatoes to a serving bowl; sprinkle with paprika. Serve warm with Cream Gravy. Yield: 8 servings.

SWEET-AND-SOUR CARROTS

2 pounds carrots, cleaned and
  cut into ½-inch slices
¼ cup plus 2 tablespoons
  firmly packed brown sugar
3 tablespoons prepared
  mustard
3 tablespoons butter or
  margarine
1 tablespoon plus 1½
  teaspoons light corn syrup
¼ teaspoon salt

Cook carrots in a small amount of boiling salted water in a medium saucepan 10 minutes or until crisp-tender; drain and set aside.

Combine remaining ingredients in a small saucepan. Cook, stirring constantly, over medium heat until butter melts.

Transfer carrots to a serving bowl; pour sauce over carrots. Toss carrots thoroughly; serve warm. Yield: 8 servings.

A satisfied turkey hunter poses for camera, c.1900.

Western Carolina University

PUMPKIN CHIFFON PIE

3 eggs, separated
1 cup sugar, divided
1¼ cups mashed, cooked
   pumpkin
½ cup milk
½ teaspoon salt
½ teaspoon ground cinnamon
½ teaspoon ground ginger
¼ teaspoon ground nutmeg
1 envelope unflavored gelatin
¼ cup cold water
½ cup chopped black walnuts
   or English walnuts
1 baked (9-inch) pastry shell,
   cooled
Whipped cream (optional)

Beat egg yolks in a medium
saucepan; add ½ cup sugar,
pumpkin, milk, and seasonings, stirring well. Cook over
low heat, stirring constantly,
until thickened and bubbly.

Soften gelatin in cold water;
let stand 5 minutes. Add to hot
mixture, stirring until gelatin
dissolves. Stir in walnuts. Let
cool; chill until mixture begins
to thicken.

Beat egg whites (at room temperature) until foamy. Gradually
add remaining sugar, beating
until stiff peaks form. Fold egg
whites into chilled pumpkin
mixture. Pour mixture into
pastry shell. Chill overnight.
Garnish with whipped cream, if
desired. Yield: one 9-inch pie.

FIRE AND ICE SALAD

6 large tomatoes, peeled and
   sliced
2 large Spanish onions, sliced
   and separated into rings
1 green pepper, seeded and
   cut into strips
1½ cups cider vinegar
½ cup water
¼ cup sugar
1 tablespoon celery seeds
1 tablespoon mustard seeds
1 teaspoon salt
½ teaspoon coarsely ground
   black pepper
Leaf lettuce

Arrange tomatoes, onions,
and green peppers in a 13- x 9- x
2-inch baking dish.

Combine vinegar, water,
sugar, celery seeds, mustard
seeds, salt, and pepper in a medium saucepan. Bring to a boil,
and boil 1 minute. Pour over
vegetables in dish. Cover and
chill overnight.

To serve, arrange marinated
vegetables attractively around
Roasted Turkey on serving platter. Yield: 8 servings.

CLOVERLEAF ROLLS

2 packages dry yeast
¼ cup plus 2 teaspoons
   sugar, divided
¼ cup warm water (105° to
   115°)
1 cup milk, scalded
¼ cup butter or margarine,
   softened
1 egg, well beaten
1 teaspoon salt
3 cups all-purpose flour
Melted butter or margarine

Combine yeast, 2 teaspoons
sugar, and water; stir. Let stand
5 minutes or until bubbly.

Combine remaining sugar,
milk, ¼ cup butter, egg, and salt
in a large mixing bowl; stir until
sugar and salt dissolve. Add
yeast mixture, stirring well. Stir
in enough flour to make a soft
dough. Cover and let rise in a
warm place (85°), free from
drafts, 1 hour or until doubled
in bulk. Punch dough down.
Cover and refrigerate at least 2
hours.

Turn dough out onto a lightly
floured surface; knead 3 or 4
times. Shape dough into 1-inch
balls; place 3 balls in each of 24
greased muffin pans. Cover and
repeat rising procedure 30 minutes or until doubled in bulk.
Bake at 400° for 10 minutes or
until lightly browned. Brush
with melted butter. Yield: 2
dozen.

THE GREAT ESCAPE

MENU OF MENUS

HORSESHOES AND A
FAMILY REUNION

AUDUBON SOCIETY
BARBECUE

BIKERS' PICNIC AT CADES
COVE

FRESH-AIR FEAST

SALT GRASS TRAIL RIDE
SUPPER

HOT-AIR BALLOON
CELEBRATION

PICNIC AFTER THE
SAVANNAH RACES

Barbecued Spareribs take center stage here, leading to molded Corn Relish Salad, Oatmeal Cake with Coconut Topping, and Green Tomato Pie: outdoor eating at its best.

In the beginning, there was work. But when the work was done, it was left behind. Life in the South was never so tough as to prevent people from throwing the business of everyday living aside and retreating to the fun and thrills of their favorite sports. Southerners of all degrees, at one time or another, have participated in an old-fashioned family reunion and, while the food was being readied, pitched horseshoes.

And bird-watchers retreat to the forests, the plains, or the seaside, armed with binoculars, hoping to focus on provocative, if not rare, species. Later, the nature lovers compare sightings and eat barbecue under the banner of famous wildlife artist John James Audubon, whose drawings "took birds out of the glass case for all time and gave them the illusion of life."

In other times and today, cycling has provided a leisurely vehicle for exploration and discovery. Even in the Great Smoky Mountains National Park, where the terrain is steep, avid bicyclers find that two-wheeling is a great way to see evidence of early settlers in Cades Cove.

The romantic, Old-West thing to do in Texas is to participate in the Salt Grass Trail Ride in the fall. Thousands of people, young and old, tycoons and mechanics, males and females, enjoy the fellowship of the arduous seventy-mile horseback ride. Around evening campfires, hungrily sharing the good chuck-wagon chow, they relive an important chapter in the state's cattle industry.

Ballooning has become more popular with each passing year. Now, even a small-town festival can afford to have a balloon-ride concession. It is thrills and chills to be in the crowd when an explosion of colorful balloons leaves the earth for a race, chasing the "hare balloon" to a marked destination. Lucky are the aeronauts; they experience the total escape, into the beauty of absolute silence.

Turn-of-the-century Savannah society dressed to the nines and, armed with wicker hampers of fancy viands, drove elegant cars to watch the Vanderbilt Cup and Grand Prize races. Whether attended in opulent style or purposefully devoid of conventional comforts, the idea is the same: to escape is to know the value of play.

HORSESHOES AND A FAMILY REUNION

Much as we run on about the elegance of the hunt in the Eastern colonies, recreation took quite a different tone on the frontier. Before the social graces were fairly mastered (or recalled) in the lands drained by the Cumberland River, Kentuckians and Tennesseans considered family reunions the primest of occasions.

They danced to fiddles, footraced, and bet on contests of strength. Horseshoe pitching was for the old and young. Crowds were fed in shifts of "tables." After the "important" folks had been served, the table was cleared and reset with clean dishes for the next shift. Even at the "last table" (where children were born to eat) the food was good.

BARBECUED SPARERIBS
GREEN TOMATO PIE
CREAMED TURNIPS
CORN RELISH SALAD
or
KIDNEY BEAN SALAD
CHOCOLATE CHIP PIE
or
OATMEAL CAKE WITH COCONUT TOPPING

Serves 6 to 8

BARBECUED SPARERIBS

8 pounds pork spareribs
2 teaspoons sugar
2 teaspoons salt
2 teaspoons pepper
1 (14-ounce) bottle catsup
¼ cup firmly packed brown sugar
¼ cup butter or margarine, melted
2 tablespoons vegetable oil
2 tablespoons Worcestershire sauce
1 tablespoon vinegar
1 tablespoon prepared mustard
⅛ teaspoon chili powder
⅛ teaspoon pepper
Dash of red pepper
Dash of garlic salt

Cut ribs into serving-size pieces. Place spareribs with water to cover in a large stockpot. Cover and bring to a boil; reduce heat, and simmer 20 minutes. Drain and cool spareribs slightly.

Combine 2 teaspoons sugar, 2 teaspoons salt, and 2 teaspoons pepper; rub over entire surface of spareribs.

Combine remaining ingredients in a small mixing bowl; mix until well blended.

Place ribs on grill 5 inches from medium-low coals. Cook 1 hour or until desired degree of doneness, turning every 20 minutes and basting liberally with barbecue sauce.

Transfer spareribs to a serving platter, and serve with remaining barbecue sauce. Yield: 6 to 8 servings.

Birthday postcard, c.1905.

GREEN TOMATO PIE

1 unbaked (9-inch) pastry shell
¾ teaspoon salt
¼ teaspoon pepper
3 medium-size green tomatoes, sliced
¾ cup all-purpose flour
¼ cup vegetable oil
1 cup chopped green onion
1 (2¼-ounce) can sliced ripe olives, drained
2 eggs, beaten
1 cup half-and-half
1 cup (4 ounces) shredded Cheddar cheese

Bake pastry shell at 450° for 8 minutes. Remove from oven; set aside.

Sprinkle salt and pepper over tomatoes; dredge in flour. Fry tomato slices in hot oil in a large skillet until browned, turning once. Drain on paper towels.

Sprinkle onion and olives in bottom of pastry shell. Arrange tomatoes over vegetables.

Combine eggs, half-and-half, and cheese, beating well. Pour over vegetables. Bake at 375° for 35 minutes or until set. Yield: one 9-inch pie.

The Swanger family reunion picnic, Grantsville, Maryland, c.1915.

CREAMED TURNIPS

3 pounds fresh turnips,
  peeled and cubed
½ cup butter or margarine
½ teaspoon salt
⅛ teaspoon pepper

Place turnips with water to cover in a small Dutch oven; bring to a boil. Cover and cook 15 minutes or until tender; drain. Mash until smooth; add butter, salt, and pepper. Transfer to a serving dish; serve immediately. Yield: 6 to 8 servings.

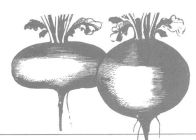

CORN RELISH SALAD

1 (3-ounce) package
  lemon-flavored gelatin
1 cup boiling water
½ cup cold water
3 tablespoons vinegar
½ teaspoon salt
1 (8¾-ounce) can whole
  kernel corn, drained
1 medium-size green pepper,
  seeded and chopped
2 tablespoons chopped
  pimiento
1 tablespoon grated
  onion
Leaf lettuce
Mayonnaise

Dissolve gelatin in boiling water; stir in cold water, vinegar, and salt. Chill until consistency of unbeaten egg white. Fold in corn, green pepper, pimiento, and onion. Spoon into a lightly oiled 4-cup mold. Chill mixture until set. Unmold salad onto a lettuce-lined serving plate, and garnish with a large dollop of mayonnaise. Yield: 6 to 8 servings.

KIDNEY BEAN SALAD

2 (15-ounce) cans kidney
  beans, drained
2 hard-cooked eggs, chopped
1 small onion, chopped
1 large stalk celery, chopped
2 tablespoons mayonnaise
2 teaspoons horseradish
  mustard

Combine beans, eggs, onion, and celery in a medium mixing bowl; mix well.

Combine mayonnaise and mustard; mix well. Add to bean mixture; toss until well coated. Chill. Yield: 6 to 8 servings.

CHOCOLATE CHIP PIE

2 tablespoons butter or
    margarine, softened
⅔ cup sugar
3 eggs, well beaten
¾ cup light corn syrup
1 tablespoon all-purpose flour
1 teaspoon vanilla extract
¼ teaspoon salt
1 unbaked (9-inch) pastry
    shell
1 (6-ounce) package
    semisweet chocolate
    morsels
1 cup sliced almonds, toasted
1 cup whipping cream,
    whipped

Cream butter in a medium mixing bowl; gradually add sugar, beating well. Add eggs, syrup, flour, vanilla, and salt; beat well.

Line the bottom of pastry shell with chocolate morsels; pour syrup mixture over chocolate morsels. Bake at 375° for 40 minutes. Sprinkle toasted almonds over top of pie, and bake an additional 15 minutes. Cool completely.

Pipe whipped cream around edge of pie, using a pastry bag. Yield: one 9-inch pie.

OATMEAL CAKE WITH COCONUT TOPPING

1¼ cups boiling water
1   cup quick-cooking oats,
     uncooked
½   cup butter or margarine
1   cup firmly packed brown
     sugar
2   eggs
1⅓ cups all-purpose flour
1   teaspoon baking soda
½   teaspoon ground cinnamon
Coconut Topping

Combine boiling water, oats, and butter in a large mixing bowl, stirring well. Let stand 20 minutes. Add sugar and eggs, beating well.

Combine flour, soda, and cinnamon; stir well. Add to oats mixture, stirring well.

Pour batter into a greased 13- x 9- x 2-inch baking pan. Bake at 350° for 25 minutes or until a wooden pick inserted in center comes out clean.

Spoon Coconut Topping over warm cake. Broil 4 inches from heating element 2 minutes or until browned. Cut into 2-inch squares. Serve warm or cold. Yield: 2 dozen.

Coconut Topping:

½ cup butter or margarine
½ cup sugar
¼ cup evaporated milk
1 cup flaked coconut
1 cup chopped pecans
1 teaspoon vanilla extract

Combine all ingredients in a small saucepan, stirring well; bring to a boil. Immediately pour hot mixture over warm cake. Yield: topping for one 13- x 9-inch cake.

Chocolate Chip Pie may be the best excuse of the year to forget about calorie counting!

A gathering of the Audubon Society in Savannah, Georgia, c.1930.

AUDUBON SOCIETY BARBECUE

In April of 1985, five hundred chapters of the Audubon Society of America celebrated John James Audubon's bicentennial with speeches and barbecues. The naturalist and painter of birds was educated in France; he came to America in 1803. At age thirty-five, he began stalking the country for species, all of which he would commit to drawings. Six years later, in 1826, he sailed for London with 435 hand-colored drawings. A publisher was quickly found, Robert Havell, Jr. It took eleven years to reproduce the drawings on copper. Some two hundred four-volume sets of *The Birds of America*, 1827-38, were printed and sold for one thousand dollars each.

BARBECUED BEEF BRISKET
BARBECUED PINTO BEANS
FRESH VEGETABLE SALAD
CARROT CUPCAKES

Serves 8

BARBECUED BEEF BRISKET

1 (4-pound) beef brisket, trimmed
Barbecue Sauce

Place brisket on grill 8 inches from low coals. Cover grill, and cook 2½ hours or until very tender, turning and basting with Barbecue Sauce every 20 minutes.

Transfer brisket to a warm platter; cut diagonally across the grain into thin slices. Serve with Barbecue Sauce. Yield: 8 servings.

Barbecue Sauce:

1 cup catsup
1 (12-ounce) bottle chili sauce
1 cup water
½ cup lemon juice
¼ cup firmly packed brown sugar
1 tablespoon Worcestershire sauce
1 tablespoon Dijon mustard
1 (1.25-ounce) package dry onion soup mix

Combine all ingredients in a medium saucepan, stirring well; bring to a boil. Reduce heat; simmer, uncovered, 10 minutes. Yield: 3¼ cups.

Note: Leftover sauce may be refrigerated for other uses.

BARBECUED PINTO BEANS

1 (16-ounce) package dried pinto beans
2 slices bacon, diced
1½ teaspoons salt
1½ cups Barbecue Sauce

Sort and wash beans; place in a large Dutch oven with water to cover 2 inches above beans; let soak 8 hours or overnight. Drain beans well.

Combine beans, bacon, and salt with water to cover 3 inches above beans. Cover and simmer 2½ hours or until beans are tender. Drain; stir in Barbecue Sauce. Simmer, uncovered, 30 minutes or until desired consistency. Yield: 8 servings.

FRESH VEGETABLE SALAD

2 cups snapped fresh green beans
2 cups shelled fresh lima beans
1 cup water
1 head iceberg lettuce, torn into bite-size pieces
12 green onions, thinly sliced
8 radishes, cleaned
2 small cucumbers, peeled and diced
2 small yellow squash, cleaned and thinly sliced
2 medium-size green peppers, seeded and chopped
1 medium carrot, scraped and thinly sliced
2 cups cauliflower flowerets
6 slices bacon
1 cup vinegar
¼ cup sugar
1 teaspoon salt
¼ teaspoon pepper

Combine green beans, lima beans, and water in a medium saucepan; cover and bring to a boil. Reduce heat, and simmer 30 minutes or until tender. Drain and chill.

Combine bean mixture, lettuce, onions, radishes, cucumbers, squash, green peppers, carrot, and cauliflower in a large mixing bowl. Toss gently; cover and chill thoroughly.

Cook bacon in a large skillet until crisp; drain on paper towels. Crumble and set aside, reserving ¼ cup drippings.

Combine reserved drippings, vinegar, sugar, salt, and pepper in a small mixing bowl, mixing well. Cover and chill thoroughly.

To serve, pour vinegar mixture over vegetable mixture, tossing to coat well. Sprinkle with reserved bacon. Yield: 8 servings.

Carrot Cupcakes for whiling away the time waiting for those birds to come within range.

CARROT CUPCAKES

2 cups all-purpose flour
2 teaspoons baking soda
1 teaspoon salt
1 tablespoon ground cinnamon
¼ teaspoon ground nutmeg
¼ teaspoon ground cloves
1⅓ cups vegetable oil
4 eggs, well beaten
2 cups sugar
3 cups grated carrots
Frosting (recipe follows)

Combine flour, soda, salt, and spices in a small mixing bowl.

Combine oil, eggs, and sugar; beat well. Add flour mixture; beat well. Stir in carrots.

Spoon batter into paper-lined muffin pans, filling only two-thirds full. Bake at 350° for 25 minutes or until cupcakes test done. Cool in pan 10 minutes; remove to wire racks to cool completely. Split each cupcake vertically through the center, leaving paper intact. Spoon 1 tablespoon frosting into each cupcake. Yield: about 3 dozen.

Frosting:

1 (8-ounce) package cream cheese, softened
½ cup butter or margarine, softened
1 (16-ounce) package powdered sugar, sifted
2 teaspoons vanilla extract

Combine cream cheese and butter; beat until light and fluffy. Gradually add sugar, beating well. Add vanilla, beating until spreading consistency. Yield: frosting for about 3 dozen cupcakes.

BIKERS' PICNIC AT CADES COVE

By 1889, pneumatic tires had been added to bicycles; even women took to cycling, discarding cumbersome dresses for harem trousers and gaiters. They took to the roads on a par with their men to pedal about the countryside. We haven't lost our desire to be at one with nature, as witnessed by the thousands who each year pack great lunches and cycle into the living past around the eleven-mile Cades Cove Loop Road in the Great Smoky Mountains. Preserved farm structures, a restored waterwheel mill, and churches and cemeteries provide a visual history of the Cove as it was in 1850, when it supported the 685 members of 132 households.

MEAL-IN-A-SANDWICH
STUFFED CELERY
DEVILED EGGS
BUTTERSCOTCH BROWNIES
FRESH WHOLE ORANGES

Serves 4 to 6

MEAL-IN-A-SANDWICH

12 slices rye bread
2 tablespoons butter or
   margarine, softened
½ pound thinly sliced, cooked
   turkey
¼ pound thinly sliced, cooked
   corned beef
1 (6-ounce) package sliced
   Swiss cheese
Almond Coleslaw

Spread 6 bread slices with butter; top each slice with turkey, corned beef, Swiss cheese, and ⅓ cup Almond Coleslaw. Cover with remaining bread slices. Yield: 4 to 6 servings.

Almond Coleslaw:

1¼ cups shredded cabbage
¼ cup finely chopped celery
¼ cup slivered almonds,
   toasted
2 tablespoons diced green
   pepper
2 tablespoons diced, peeled
   cucumber
1 tablespoon plus 1½
   teaspoons minced onion
¼ cup mayonnaise
½ teaspoon sugar
½ teaspoon vinegar
⅛ teaspoon salt

Combine all ingredients; toss lightly. Chill overnight. Drain well. Yield: about 4 cups.

Meal-in-a-Sandwich, Deviled Eggs, and oranges.

The John P. Cable Mill in Cades Cove provided settlers with cornmeal.

STUFFED CELERY

1 bunch celery
1 (3-ounce) package cream
 cheese, softened
1 tablespoon mayonnaise
3 drops Worcestershire sauce
Dash of salt
⅛ teaspoon pepper
⅛ teaspoon paprika
Additional paprika

Cut off base of celery, and separate into stalks. Wash under cold water, using a stiff brush. Cut 6 inner stalks into 2-inch pieces (reserve remaining outer stalks for other uses). Set celery pieces aside.

Combine cream cheese, mayonnaise, Worcestershire sauce, salt, pepper, and ⅛ teaspoon paprika in a small mixing bowl; beat until well blended. Stuff celery pieces with cream cheese mixture. Chill. Sprinkle with additional paprika. Yield: 4 to 6 servings.

DEVILED EGGS

8 hard-cooked eggs
¼ cup salad dressing
1 tablespoon finely chopped
 sweet pickle
¼ teaspoon salt
¼ teaspoon paprika

Slice eggs in half lengthwise; remove yolks. Combine yolks and salad dressing; mash well. Stir in pickle, salt, and paprika. Stuff half of egg whites liberally with yolk mixture. Top with remaining egg whites, pressing gently. Wrap in plastic wrap. Chill. Yield: 4 to 6 servings.

BUTTERSCOTCH BROWNIES

½ cup butter or margarine,
 melted
1½ cups firmly packed dark
 brown sugar
2 eggs
1 teaspoon vanilla
1½ cups all-purpose flour
2 teaspoons baking powder
½ teaspoon salt
¾ cup chopped pecans

Combine butter and sugar in a large mixing bowl, mixing well. Add eggs and vanilla; beat until well blended.

Sift together flour, baking powder, and salt in a small mixing bowl. Gradually add to creamed mixture, stirring well. Stir in pecans. Spread mixture in a greased 9-inch square pan. Bake at 350° for 30 minutes. Cool brownies completely in pan, and cut into 1½-inch squares. Yield: 3 dozen.

FRESH AIR FEAST

Camping may owe some of its perennial popularity to a nostalgia for our ancestral days, when life itself was one long, sometimes brutally hard, camping trip. Our range is broader now; we may drive to a campsite, or we may boat, hike, or cycle to it. Especially made for the camper who must carry every amenity along are the lightweight kits of cookware, usually aluminum, and the wee camp stove. Backpackers and bicycle trippers sometimes opt for the camping stove instead of the campfire because it is more reliable. Even the traditionalist welcomes the innovation when rain prevents a bona fide campfire. Often the hot food is what counts!

CAMPERS' STEW
ASSORTED RAW VEGETABLES
GRILLED GARLIC BREAD
TOASTED COCONUT SQUARES
SPICED ORANGE JUICE

Serves 4

CAMPERS' STEW

1 pound ground chuck
1 teaspoon salt
½ teaspoon pepper
1 medium onion, thinly sliced
1 medium potato, peeled and thinly sliced
2 carrots, scraped and thinly sliced
Salt and pepper to taste

Combine ground chuck, 1 teaspoon salt, and ½ teaspoon pepper; mix well, and form into 4 patties.

Place each beef patty on a 12-x 9-inch sheet of heavy-duty aluminum foil. Top each patty with sliced onion, potato, and carrots; sprinkle with salt and pepper to taste. Wrap foil around meat and vegetables, and seal securely.

Place aluminum foil-wrapped dinners, sealed side down, 3 inches from hot coals. Turn packages after 10 minutes, and cook an additional 20 minutes or until vegetables are tender when pierced with a fork. Yield: 4 servings.

Note: Recipe may be easily adapted to yield a single serving.

An idea for outdoorsmen:
Campers' Stew and
Toasted Coconut Squares.

Campfire Girls living up to their name in Florida, circa 1930.

GRILLED GARLIC BREAD

½ cup butter or margarine
1 clove garlic, crushed
1 (1-pound) loaf commercial
French bread

Melt butter in a small saucepan, and stir in crushed garlic. Cut bread into thick slices, and spread each slice with garlic butter. Stack slices into a loaf; wrap in aluminum foil, and place on back of grill 20 minutes, turning loaf often. Serve hot. Yield: 4 servings.

TOASTED COCONUT SQUARES

1 (10-ounce) commercial
angel food cake, cut into
2-inch cubes
1 (14-ounce) can sweetened
condensed milk
3 cups flaked coconut

Dip each piece of cake into milk, and roll in coconut. Place squares on long-handled forks or skewers, and toast over medium-low coals until golden brown. Serve warm. Yield: 4 servings.

SPICED ORANGE JUICE

2 cups apple cider
½ teaspoon ground allspice
½ teaspoon ground cinnamon
¼ teaspoon ground nutmeg
¼ cup sugar
1½ quarts chilled orange
juice

Combine cider and spices in a medium saucepan. Bring to a boil. Remove from heat, and stir in sugar. Cool. Add orange juice; store in an insulated container. Yield: 2 quarts.

SALT GRASS TRAIL RIDE SUPPER

Early cattlemen knew (long before research verified it) that the fifteen-mile-wide band of salt grass extending from Orange to Brownsville along the Gulf Coast of Texas made cattle fat and healthy; stockmen drove herds there to graze from November through February. One cold day in 1952, Reese Lockett, the mayor of Brenham, was commiserating with some pals about their plane being weathered in on a previous trip. "I'll never make another trip where I can't ride home on my horse," Reese said. So was born the idea of the seventy-mile Salt Grass Trail Ride from Brenham to Houston, which has become the largest organized horseback ride of modern times. Chuck wagons accompany the thousands of riders, feeding them like kings as they make for the opening of the Houston Fat Stock Show.

BIG-BATCH BEEF STEW
FRUIT SALAD
GORP
CRACKLING CORNBREAD

Serves 20

BIG-BATCH BEEF STEW

6 pounds lean beef for stewing, cut into 1-inch cubes
6 large onions, chopped
3 pounds carrots, scraped and cut into ½-inch slices
3 cloves garlic, crushed
3 cups water
2 tablespoons Worcestershire sauce
2 teaspoons salt
½ teaspoon pepper
1 teaspoon dried whole thyme
2 bay leaves
4 pounds potatoes, peeled and cubed
1 (29-ounce) can tomato sauce
1 (12-ounce) can beer

Brown meat in a large stockpot over medium heat. Add onion; sauté until tender. Stir in carrots, garlic, water, Worcestershire sauce, and seasonings; bring to a boil. Reduce heat; cover and simmer 1 hour.

Add potatoes, tomato sauce, and beer; stir well. Simmer, uncovered, 1 hour or until vegetables are tender. Discard bay leaves. Yield: 2 gallons.

FRUIT SALAD

3 cups watermelon balls
3 cups cantaloupe balls
3 cups honeydew balls
3 cups fresh pineapple chunks
3 cups sliced, peeled fresh peaches
3 cups seedless white grapes

Combine all ingredients; toss lightly to distribute evenly. Chill. Yield: 20 servings.

GORP

3 cups quick-cooking oats, uncooked
½ cup peanuts
½ cup flaked coconut
¾ cup honey
1 tablespoon plus 1½ teaspoons vegetable oil
1 cup candy-coated milk chocolate pieces
½ cup raisins
¾ cup chopped dried fruit

Combine first 5 ingredients; stir. Spread in a greased 15- x 10- x 1-inch jellyroll pan. Bake at 300° for 30 minutes, stirring every 15 minutes. Transfer to a mixing bowl to cool. Break into small pieces. Stir in remaining ingredients. Yield: 6 cups.

CRACKLING CORNBREAD

3 cups cornmeal
1 cup all-purpose flour
1 teaspoon salt
1 teaspoon baking soda
3 cups buttermilk
4 eggs, beaten
¼ cup vegetable oil
3 cups cracklings
Butter

Sift together cornmeal, flour, and salt in a large mixing bowl.

Dissolve soda in buttermilk; add to flour mixture, stirring until well blended.

Add eggs, oil, and cracklings, stirring just until dry ingredients are moistened.

Pour batter into a well-greased 10½-inch cast-iron skillet. Bake at 350° for 15 minutes. Increase temperature to 425°, and bake an additional 25 minutes or until lightly browned. Cut into wedges, and serve warm with butter. Yield: about 20 servings.

Beef Stew is the camper's best friend when cooked in embers and served on Crackling Cornbread.

HOT-AIR BALLOON CELEBRATION

Man's fascination with lighter-than-air vehicles goes back to the Middle Ages, but it was the Montgolfier brothers of France who put the first man, physicist Pilâtre De Rozier, aloft in 1783. De Rozier's own attempt, in 1785, to combine the Montgolfière (fire balloon) with a hydrogen balloon met with a fiery disaster that took his life. Balloons have since been used for spying in wartime and for weather predicting; the shape even influenced women's styles. Interest in ballooning continues to spread. Racing is popular, with the "hare balloon" being chased by the "hounds"; crewing is now a hobby/pastime, as is partying afterward.

HERBED CHEESE HEART
SHRIMP ROLLS
MARINATED TOMATO SALAD
FRESH PEACH CAKE
CHAMPAGNE

Serves 4

HERBED CHEESE HEART

1 (8-ounce) package cream cheese, softened
2 tablespoons commercial sour cream
1 clove garlic, crushed
¼ teaspoon crushed basil leaves
¼ teaspoon dried whole thyme
⅓ cup finely chopped pecans
Assorted crackers

Beat cream cheese in a small mixing bowl until light and fluffy; add sour cream, garlic, basil, and thyme, mixing until well blended. Cover mixture, and chill thoroughly.

Turn mixture out onto a serving platter; shape into a heart. Press pecans into heart. Cover and chill. Serve with crackers. Yield: 4 servings.

Get carried away with Shrimp Rolls, Marinated Tomato Salad, and Fresh Peach Cake.

SHRIMP ROLLS

1 quart water
2 teaspoons salt
½ pound medium uncooked
   shrimp
1 cup shredded Bibb lettuce
¼ cup chopped celery
¼ cup chopped cucumber
1 tablespoon chopped fresh
   parsley
1 teaspoon minced
   onion
¼ cup mayonnaise
½ teaspoon salt
¼ teaspoon pepper
4 large hard rolls
1 tablespoon butter or
   margarine, softened
Fresh parsley sprigs

Combine water and 2 teaspoons salt in a large saucepan. Cover and bring to a boil. Add shrimp; cook, uncovered, 3 minutes. (Do not boil.) Drain; rinse in cold water. Peel and devein shrimp; set aside 4 shrimp. Chop remaining shrimp.

Combine chopped shrimp, lettuce, celery, cucumber, chopped parsley, onion, mayonnaise, ¼ teaspoon salt, and pepper in a medium mixing bowl; stir well to blend. Cover with plastic wrap, and chill.

To serve, spread partially split hard rolls with softened butter. Fill each roll with one-fourth of chilled shrimp mixture. Transfer shrimp rolls to a serving platter, and garnish with reserved shrimp and parsley sprigs. Yield: 4 servings.

The forerunner of the blimp, displayed at an exhibition, c.1925.

MARINATED TOMATO SALAD

½ cup olive oil
3 tablespoons vinegar
2 tablespoons chopped
   green onion
1 tablespoon sugar
1 teaspoon dried whole basil
1 teaspoon Worcestershire
   sauce
¾ teaspoon salt
⅛ teaspoon pepper
Dash of ground thyme
1 small clove garlic, crushed
2 large tomatoes, peeled and
   sliced
Red leaf lettuce

Combine all ingredients, except tomatoes and lettuce, in a medium mixing bowl; stir until well combined. Add tomatoes; toss gently to coat well. Cover with plastic wrap, and refrigerate at least 1 hour.

Arrange tomatoes on individual lettuce-lined plates. Serve chilled. Yield: 4 servings.

FRESH PEACH CAKE

2 cups all-purpose flour
1 teaspoon baking powder
1 teaspoon salt
1 teaspoon grated lemon rind
3 eggs, well beaten
1¾ cups sugar, divided
1 cup vegetable oil
3 cups sliced, peeled fresh
   peaches
½ cup chopped pecans
Vanilla ice cream
Additional peach slices

Combine first 4 ingredients; mix well.

Combine eggs, 1½ cups sugar, and oil; beat until smooth. Add flour mixture; beat until blended. Pour batter in a greased and floured 13- x 9- x 2-inch baking pan.

Combine 3 cups peaches and remaining sugar. Arrange peaches on top of batter; sprinkle pecans over top. Bake at 350° for 1 hour and 15 minutes or until cake tests done. Cool 10 minutes. Cut into 3-inch squares. Serve with ice cream and additional peach slices. Yield: one 13- x 9-inch cake.

PICNIC AFTER THE SAVANNAH RACES

Savannah native and New York social leader Ward McAllister (1827-1895), who compiled a list of New York's prominent "Four Hundred," referred to his hometown as "Little New York." Belles in extravagant gowns danced the waltz and turkey trot at splendid balls, and fashionable families took box seats and picnics to two of the most exclusive social events of the times: the Grand Prize and Vanderbilt Cup races. After the races, which attracted European drivers and cars, chic spectators retreated to a more pastoral setting, where they picnicked on fried chicken and champagne, served up with fine china and silver on white damask.

BUTTERMILK FRIED CHICKEN
SAVANNAH SALAD
HERBED FRENCH BREAD
CHILLED CUSTARD SAUCE OVER
STRAWBERRIES AND RASPBERRIES
ALMOND LACE WAFERS
ICED TEA
CHAMPAGNE

Serves 4 to 6

BUTTERMILK FRIED CHICKEN

1 (3- to 3½-pound)
   broiler-fryer, cut up
½ cup buttermilk
1 cup all-purpose flour
1½ teaspoons salt
½ teaspoon ground thyme
½ teaspoon ground marjoram
½ teaspoon paprika
⅛ teaspoon pepper
Vegetable oil

Place chicken in a shallow pan; pour buttermilk over chicken. Combine flour and seasonings in a plastic or paper bag; shake to mix. Place 2 or 3 pieces of chicken in bag; shake well. Repeat procedure with remaining chicken.

Heat ½ inch of oil in a large skillet to 350°; add chicken, and fry 20 minutes or until golden brown, turning once. Drain well. Yield: 4 to 6 servings.

Pack this classy picnic: Buttermilk Fried Chicken, Savannah Salad, and Herbed French Bread.

Joe Dawson, shown with Governor Joe Brown, won the Savannah Challenge trophy, 1910.

SAVANNAH SALAD

1 head Boston lettuce, torn
1 large bunch leaf lettuce,
   torn
4 hard-cooked eggs
¼ cup chopped toasted
   pecans
Butter-Toasted Croutons
Savannah Dressing

Place lettuce in a salad bowl. Press eggs through a sieve. Sprinkle eggs, pecans, and Butter-Toasted Croutons over lettuce. Serve with Savannah Dressing. Yield: 4 to 6 servings.

Butter-Toasted Croutons:

4 slices bread, crust
   removed
¼ cup olive oil
¼ cup butter or margarine
1 clove garlic,
   minced

Cut bread slices into ⅜-inch cubes. Combine oil, butter, and garlic in a small skillet; place over medium heat. Drop bread cubes into hot oil mixture, and cook, stirring occasionally, until lightly browned. Remove with a slotted spoon; drain. Yield: about 2 cups.

Savannah Dressing:

¼ cup olive oil
¼ cup vegetable oil
¼ cup red wine vinegar
1 tablespoon water
1 small onion, minced
1 clove garlic, minced
1 teaspoon grated Parmesan
   cheese
1 teaspoon ground oregano
1 teaspoon salt
½ teaspoon white pepper

Combine all ingredients in a jar; cover and shake vigorously. Chill. Shake well before serving. Yield: 1 cup.

HERBED FRENCH BREAD

1 package dry yeast
1 cup warm water (105° to 115°)
2 teaspoons sugar
1 teaspoon salt
1 teaspoon marjoram leaves
¾ teaspoon dried whole dill
¾ teaspoon dried whole thyme
½ teaspoon dried rosemary
1 tablespoon shortening
3 cups all-purpose flour
¼ cup butter or margarine, melted
Poppy seeds

Dissolve yeast in water in a small mixing bowl. Let stand 5 minutes or until bubbly.

Combine sugar, salt, marjoram, dill, thyme, and rosemary in a large mixing bowl; mix well. Add shortening and dissolved yeast, stirring well. Gradually add flour, stirring until dough leaves sides of bowl. Let rest 10 minutes.

Turn dough out onto a lightly floured surface; knead 5 minutes or until smooth and elastic. Place dough in a greased bowl, turning to grease top. Cover and let rise in a warm place (85°), free from drafts, 1½ hours or until doubled in bulk.

Punch dough down; turn out onto a floured surface. Cover loosely with plastic wrap or cheesecloth, and let rest 10 minutes. Divide dough in half. Roll each half into a 12- x 9-inch rectangle. Roll up each rectangle jellyroll fashion, starting at long end. Pinch seams and ends together to seal. Place loaves, seam side down, in 2 heavily greased baguette pans. (Baking sheets may be used instead of baguette pans.)

Cut 6 diagonal slashes, ¾-inch deep, in each loaf. Cover and repeat rising procedure 1 hour or until doubled in bulk. Bake at 425° for 20 minutes or until loaves sound hollow when tapped. Brush with butter; sprinkle with poppy seeds. Bake an additional 5 minutes. Remove from pans; cool on wire racks. Yield: 2 loaves.

CHILLED CUSTARD SAUCE OVER STRAWBERRIES AND RASPBERRIES

3 cups half-and-half
3 eggs
1 cup sugar
2 tablespoons cornstarch
1 teaspoon vanilla extract
1 pint fresh strawberries, washed and hulled
1 pint fresh raspberries, washed

Scald half-and-half in top of a double boiler over boiling water.

Beat eggs in a medium mixing bowl until light and fluffy. Combine sugar and cornstarch; add to eggs, beating well. Gradually stir one-third of warm half-and-half into egg mixture; add to remaining half-and-half in top of double boiler, stirring well.

Cook over boiling water, stirring until mixture thickens and coats a spoon. Remove from heat; stir in vanilla. Cool completely; chill thoroughly. Spoon over strawberries and raspberries in individual serving dishes. Yield: 4 to 6 servings.

ALMOND LACE WAFERS

½ cup butter or margarine, softened
⅔ cup sifted powdered sugar
½ teaspoon almond extract
½ cup plus 2 tablespoons all-purpose flour
1 egg white
Sliced almonds

Cream butter in a medium mixing bowl; add sugar and almond extract, beating until light and fluffy. Gradually add flour, beating well.

Beat egg white (at room temperature) in a small mixing bowl until stiff peaks form; gently fold into creamed mixture.

Drop dough by heaping ½ teaspoonfuls 1½ inches apart onto greased cookie sheets. Place an almond slice on top of each, and bake at 375° for 8 minutes or until edges are golden brown. Allow cookies to stand 1 minute on cookie sheets before transferring to wire racks to cool completely. Store cookies in airtight containers. Yield: about 4 dozen.

The Vanderbilt Cup races moved from Rhode Island to wealthy, sporting Savannah in 1910. They had been sponsored by the American Automobile Association until a rift occurred in 1908. That year the Automobile Club of America sponsored the American Grand Prize. It, too, was held near Savannah, one month after the Vanderbilt Cup. The first event attracted top European drivers, eager to master the tortuous 402-mile course. Louis Wagner, a Frenchman on the Darracq team, won the Grand Prize in his Fiat. No races occurred in 1909, but the 1910 and 1911 Savannah races were *Formule Libre* events; cars of unlimited capacity were accepted. Those years brought many thrills, many firsts! Racing pioneer Ralph Mulford, whose religious convictions kept him from racing on Sundays, secured the 1911 national driving championship and, as if that were too little, rammed his standard model Lozier down the 291-mile Vanderbilt Cup course to set a speed record of 74.21 mph.

The Grand Stand.
Grand Prize and
Vanderbilt Cup Race,
Savannah, Ga.

START FINISH

OFFICIAL PROGRAM and SCORE CARD of the VANDERBILT CUP and GRAND PRIZE RACES

also Savannah and Tiedeman Trophy Races

under the auspices Savannah Automobile Club

to be held at Savannah Ga.

November 27th and 30th 1911

PRICE 25 CENTS

Changing a tire during the 1912 races.

Racing mementos include 1908 picture of French driver Wagner.

THE WATER'S EDGE

Feasting on fresh seafood at water's edge is one of the oldest American traditions. The Puritans landed on shores where the Indians had perfected the clambake. And oyster roasts, as well as crab feasts, were adapted by our own European forebears, having learned about them from the Southern Indians. Picnics and cook-outs along the shore have since increased in popularity — simultaneously with innovations in water sports.

Organized regattas and other boat races probably began with the old "canoe boats" with which the first aquatic clubs were organized in Georgia. These were patterned after the Indian dugout and powered by four or six oarsmen. Nowadays crowds, sitting on the seawall in Annapolis, Maryland, watch as midshipmen in varnished shells head for the creeks surrounding the Naval Academy. Eight men row, slicing through the water to the call of "Stroke!" "Stroke!" Crewing has been a source of pride at the Academy since the 1870s. But it was sailing ships, with sails evolved from ancient Mediterranean craft, that brought the early settlers. Inevitably sailboats were built to be used as fast, light racers for the sporting set. Parties at the boathouse usually follow regattas, with good fixings for sunburned sailors.

The freshwater angler cares not for speed at all. At most, he will rev up the electric outboard on his dinghy in pursuit of clear waters, active with bass or trout. He does not have to be told to dress his catch and commit it to the frying pan as soon as the dry land can be reached. His waterside dinner is every bit as tasty as the seaside dweller's, his trusty ice chest just as full of cold liquid refreshment.

Modern boats that take sport fishermen out from Pensacola and other coastal cities are equipped with powerful motors for finding trophy-sized billfish in deep blue water. And when it comes to marlin, Floridians have found out how to make a feast of it when they return to shore. One seven-foot marlin will feed the multitudes.

Whether we sail, fish, or just plunge into a local creek on an August afternoon, the water's edge goes hand-in-hand with something good to eat, and the menus in this chapter include "carry-alongs." But first decide: will it be a harvest from the sea or wieners to roast over a campfire?

MENU OF MENUS

THE REGATTA
BOATHOUSE SUPPER

CRAB FEAST AFTER THE
RACE

WIENER ROAST BY THE
SWIMMING HOLE

AT THE BEACH IN
ST. AUGUSTINE

BEACH PARTY ON SANTA
ROSA ISLAND

FISHERMEN'S LAKESIDE
SUPPER

GAME FISH CELEBRATION
IN PENSACOLA

Get ready, get set for after the regatta! Corn Grilled in Husks (front), Pork Tenderloins, Cold Bean Salad with Coleslaw, and Grilled Garlic Bread: a winning cook-it-on-the-grill menu.

Portsmouth Yacht Racing Association's regatta, Norfolk, 1947.

THE REGATTA BOATHOUSE SUPPER

In 1834, young Georgia planters started racing "canoe boats" dug out of a single cypress and powered by four or six oarsmen. Two years later, they founded The Aquatic Club of Georgia and issued a challenge to any New York boat club to race one of their four-oared "plank boats" against the proud canoe boat *Lizard*. No takers. In 1838, the Lower Creek Boat Club of Savannah bought a New York plank boat and challenged The Aquatic Club. Some folks mortgaged their homes for betting money. The prize was the losing boat; the Aquatic Club took home the plank craft.

PORK TENDERLOINS
CORN GRILLED IN HUSKS
COLD BEAN SALAD
COLESLAW
GRILLED GARLIC BREAD
LEMON-GLAZED CHESS BARS
ITALIAN CREAM CAKE
ICED TEA

Serves 8

PORK TENDERLOINS

1 cup soy sauce
½ cup butter or margarine, melted
3 tablespoons honey
3 tablespoons red wine vinegar
1 tablespoon dry mustard
1 clove garlic, minced
4 (¾-pound) pork tenderloins

Combine all ingredients, except tenderloins, in a small mixing bowl; mix well. Set aside.

Trim excess fat from tenderloins. Place tenderloins in a shallow baking dish; pour marinade over meat. Cover and marinate 24 hours in refrigerator, turning occasionally.

Transfer meat to a greased shallow roasting pan; reserve marinade. Bake, uncovered, at 325° for 20 to 25 minutes.

Transfer meat to grill, and insert meat thermometer into thickest part of tenderloin. Grill over medium coals 30 minutes, turning and basting tenderloins occasionally with reserved marinade. Meat is done when meat thermometer registers 170°. Remove tenderloins to a large serving platter; slice and serve warm. Yield: 8 servings.

CORN GRILLED IN HUSKS

8 ears fresh corn in husks
Butter or margarine
Salt and pepper to taste

Place corn in a large container with cold water to cover; soak 1 hour. Remove from water; drain.

Place corn on grill. Cover and cook over medium coals 35 minutes or until corn is tender, turning ears frequently. Remove husks; serve with butter. Season with salt and pepper to taste. Yield: 8 servings.

Nineteenth-century trade card: a little girl, close to inventing the hula hoop, distracted by a schooner.

COLD BEAN SALAD

1 (16-ounce) can French-style green beans, well drained
1 (16-ounce) can cut green beans, well drained
1 (16-ounce) can wax beans, well drained
1 (15-ounce) can red kidney beans, well drained
1 cup chopped onion
½ cup chopped red or green pepper
1 cup vinegar
⅓ cup vegetable oil
½ cup sugar
1 teaspoon salt
½ teaspoon pepper

Combine first 6 ingredients in a large bowl; toss lightly.

Combine vinegar, oil, sugar, salt, and pepper in a small mixing bowl, stirring well. Pour over beans; mix lightly. Cover and marinate in refrigerator overnight. Yield: 8 servings.

COLESLAW

1 medium cabbage, shredded
¾ cup salad dressing
⅔ cup chopped onion
½ cup sugar
2 teaspoons celery seeds
Paprika

Combine all ingredients, except paprika, in a large mixing bowl; mix well. Sprinkle with paprika. Serve chilled. Yield: 8 servings.

GRILLED GARLIC BREAD

3 tablespoons butter, softened
1 teaspoon garlic powder
1 (½-pound) loaf French bread

Combine butter and garlic powder in a small bowl; stir until well blended. Split French bread in half lengthwise, and spread each cut side with butter mixture.

Place bread, cut side down, on grill. Grill 2 minutes and 30 seconds over medium coals or until golden brown. Turn bread, and grill an additional 2 minutes and 30 seconds. Cut into ¾-inch slices, and serve hot. Yield: 8 servings.

LEMON-GLAZED CHESS BARS

1 cup plus 2 tablespoons all-purpose flour, divided
2 tablespoons sugar
½ cup butter or margarine, melted
1 cup firmly packed dark brown sugar
1 tablespoon baking powder
1 cup chopped pecans
2 eggs, beaten
1 cup sifted powdered sugar
1 tablespoon lemon juice
1 teaspoon vanilla extract

Combine 1 cup flour and 2 tablespoons sugar in a small mixing bowl; add melted butter, mixing well. Press mixture evenly into a 13- x 9- x 2-inch baking pan. Bake at 375° for 10 minutes.

Combine brown sugar, remaining 2 tablespoons flour, baking powder, chopped pecans, and eggs in a medium mixing bowl, beating until well blended. Pour over baked crust. Bake at 350° for 30 minutes. Let cool slightly.

Combine powdered sugar, lemon juice, and vanilla in a small mixing bowl; stir well. Spread over cake. Cut into 3- x 1½-inch bars. Yield: about 2 dozen.

Tall, handsome Italian Cream Cake.

ITALIAN CREAM CAKE

½ cup butter or margarine, softened
½ cup shortening
2 cups sugar
5 eggs, separated
2 cups all-purpose flour
1 teaspoon baking soda
1 cup buttermilk
1 teaspoon vanilla extract
1 (3½-ounce) can flaked coconut
1 cup chopped pecans
Frosting (recipe follows)
Additional chopped pecans

Cream butter and shortening in a large mixing bowl; add sugar, beating well. Add egg yolks, and beat well.

Combine flour and soda. Add to creamed mixture alternately with buttermilk, beginning and ending with flour mixture. Mix well. Stir in vanilla, coconut, and 1 cup pecans.

Beat egg whites (at room temperature) in a medium mixing bowl until stiff peaks form. Gently fold egg whites into batter. Spoon batter into 3 greased and floured 9-inch round cakepans. Bake at 350° for 25 minutes or until a wooden pick inserted in center comes out clean. Cool in pans 10 minutes; remove layers from pans, and let cool completely.

Spread frosting between layers and on top and sides of cake. Sprinkle additional pecans over top. Slice and serve. Yield: one 3-layer cake.

Frosting:

1 (8-ounce) package cream cheese, softened
½ cup butter or margarine, softened
5 cups sifted powdered sugar

Combine cream cheese and butter in a large mixing bowl; beat until creamy. Gradually add powdered sugar, beating until well blended. Use immediately. Yield: frosting for one 3-layer cake.

CRAB FEAST AFTER THE RACE

On any fair day from spring to fall, bobbing armadas of sailboats are on Chesapeake Bay. Clubs in the Bay region of Delaware, Maryland, and Virginia sponsor regattas. Friends vie one-on-one, perhaps with a little betting on the side: a Southern tradition. The beauty of utter silence, as in ballooning, is one of the lures of this graceful sport. It is also a powerful appetite-building exercise. Weekend sailors know the treatment: a crab feast ashore when the race is over. Great tubfuls of hard crabs, steamed and dumped unceremoniously onto newspapers, are attacked with mallets and knives until satiety sets in. Most drink cold beer.

PECAN CHEESE BALL
STEAMED CRABS
COCKTAIL SAUCE
COLD ROAST BEEF SALAD
VEGETABLE CASSEROLE
BOURBON-BLAZED PEACHES OVER
FROZEN CUSTARD
ICED TEA
BEER

Serves 6 to 8

Fun isn't a modern invention: two-men-in-a-tub race, c.1890.

PECAN CHEESE BALL

1 (8-ounce) package cream
  cheese, softened
¼ pound blue cheese,
  crumbled
½ cup (2 ounces) shredded
  sharp Cheddar cheese
2 tablespoons minced
  onion
1½ teaspoons Worcestershire
  sauce
½ cup finely chopped pecans
Assorted crackers

Combine first 5 ingredients in
a medium mixing bowl; mix
well. Shape into a ball, and roll
in chopped pecans. Chill well.
Serve with assorted crackers.
Yield: one 4-inch cheese ball.

Note: Make cheese ball several
days in advance for full flavor. It
may also be frozen.

STEAMED CRABS

1 quart water
2 cups vinegar
2 tablespoons dry mustard
2 tablespoons pepper
2 teaspoons red pepper
2 teaspoons coriander seeds
3 to 4 dozen live blue crabs

Combine water, vinegar, mustard, pepper, and coriander in a
large stockpot with a tight fit-
ting lid, stirring until well combined. Place a rack in the
bottom of the stockpot, and
bring mixture to a boil. Add
crabs; cover and steam 20 minutes or until crabs turn bright
red in color.

Remove crabs to a large platter; serve with Cocktail Sauce.
Yield: 6 to 8 servings.

COCKTAIL SAUCE

1 cup catsup
¼ cup plus 2 tablespoons
  lemon juice
2 tablespoons prepared
  horseradish
1 tablespoon plus 1 teaspoon
  Worcestershire sauce
4 drops hot sauce
½ teaspoon salt
⅛ teaspoon celery salt

Combine all ingredients in a
small mixing bowl; stir until
well blended. Cover and chill
thoroughly. Transfer to a serving dish, and serve with
Steamed Crabs or other seafood. Yield: about 1⅓ cups.

COLD ROAST BEEF SALAD

1⅓ cups vegetable oil
2 teaspoons grated lemon
  rind
⅔ cup lemon juice
2 teaspoons Worcestershire
  sauce
2 teaspoons prepared
  mustard
½ teaspoon salt
1 pound rare roast beef or
  leftover steak, thinly sliced
  and cut into bite-size pieces
12 cups romaine or leaf
  lettuce, torn into bite-size
  pieces
½ pound Swiss cheese, cut
  into ¼-inch strips
½ cup chopped green pepper
¼ cup chopped green onion

Combine first 6 ingredients in
a jar. Cover tightly, and shake
jar vigorously. Place beef in a
shallow dish; pour lemon mixture over beef. Cover and refrigerate at least 3 hours.

To serve, combine lettuce,
cheese, green pepper, onion,
and beef mixture in a large salad
bowl; toss lightly. Yield: 6 to 8
servings.

Atlanta Historical Society

*Something delicious about
to happen here as man
tends steaming kettle of
fresh crab, c.1900.*

VEGETABLE CASSEROLE

1 (10-ounce) package frozen sweet peas
1 (10-ounce) package frozen cut green beans
1 (10-ounce) package frozen lima beans
1 (4.5-ounce) jar sliced mushrooms, drained
1 medium-size green pepper, seeded and chopped
1 (3-ounce) can grated Parmesan cheese
1 cup mayonnaise
1 cup whipped cream

Cook peas and beans separately according to package directions; drain well. Layer peas, beans, mushrooms, pepper, and cheese in a 12- x 8- x 2-inch baking dish. Repeat layers, reserving ½ cup cheese.

Combine mayonnaise and whipped cream; spread evenly over top of vegetable layers. Sprinkle with reserved cheese. Bake at 350° for 20 minutes or until browned and puffed. Yield: 6 to 8 servings.

BOURBON-BLAZED PEACHES OVER FROZEN CUSTARD

3 tablespoons butter or margarine
1 teaspoon grated orange rind
6 firm, ripe peaches, peeled and sliced
2 tablespoons orange marmalade
1 tablespoon sugar
1 tablespoon lemon juice
½ cup bourbon
Frozen Custard

Melt butter in a large skillet over medium heat; stir in orange rind. Add peaches, orange marmalade, sugar, and lemon juice, stirring well. Cook over medium heat, stirring frequently, until peaches are tender.

Place bourbon in a small saucepan; cook until thoroughly heated. (Do not boil.)

Bourbon-Blazed Peaches over Frozen Custard.

Pour over peach mixture, and ignite with a long match; stir until flames die down. Serve immediately over Frozen Vanilla Custard in individual bowls. Yield: 6 to 8 servings.

Frozen Custard:

2 quarts milk
8 eggs, beaten
1 cup sugar
2 teaspoons vanilla extract

Combine all ingredients in a large Dutch oven; beat with a wire whisk until well blended. Cook over medium-low heat, stirring constantly, 20 minutes or until mixture thickens and coats a metal spoon. Remove from heat, and cool slightly.

Pour mixture into freezer can of a 1-gallon hand-turned or electric freezer. Freeze according to manufacturer's instructions. Let custard ripen at least 1 hour before serving. Yield: about 1 gallon.

Note: Additional milk may be added to freezer can if mixture does not reach fill line.

WIENER ROAST BY THE SWIMMING HOLE

In the days before swimming pools became commonplace, every inland community had a favorite swimming hole. It may have been a clear, deep spot in a creek near a forgotten bridge, a protected curve in a stream, or a crystalline lake or pond. Seaside dwellers were never wanting for a place to swim; they simply took to the beaches when weather permitted and assumed the water would be fine. Styles in bathing wear have undergone some changes since the days of the old swimming hole, but going for a wiener roast is still possible, if you know of a natural swimming hole where trees overhang the water and rocks crop out for sunbathers and turtles.

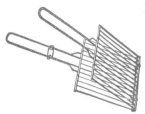

FRANKFURTERS WITH CONDIMENTS
CAMPFIRE PORK AND BEANS
POTATO CHIPS
DILL PICKLES
S'MORES

Serves 6

Nothing tastes better than frankfurters cooked over a fire; add Campfire Pork and Beans and S'Mores.

FRANKFURTERS WITH CONDIMENTS

12 beef frankfurters
12 frankfurter buns
Prepared mustard
Mayonnaise
Catsup
1 cup sweet pickle relish
1 medium onion, chopped
1 (8-ounce) package extra sharp Cheddar cheese, shredded
1 (15½-ounce) can chili without beans (optional)

Grill frankfurters over hot coals, turning frequently, until browned.

Spread buns with small amounts of mustard, mayonnaise, and catsup. Add frankfurters; top with small amounts of pickle relish, onion, and cheese. Heat chili thoroughly, and spoon over frankfurters, if desired. Yield: 6 servings.

CAMPFIRE PORK AND BEANS

2 (16-ounce) cans pork and beans
¼ cup plus 2 tablespoons firmly packed brown sugar
1 teaspoon Worcestershire sauce
1 teaspoon prepared mustard
2 slices bacon, chopped

Combine all ingredients, mixing well; spoon into an airtight container to carry to campsite. Pour beans into a heavy skillet. Cook over hot coals 10 minutes or until hot and bubbly. Yield: 6 servings.

Around 1900, these boys knew how to beat the summer's heat with a dip in the old swimming hole.

S'MORES

6 (1.45-ounce) bars milk chocolate, halved
12 graham crackers, halved
12 large marshmallows

Place chocolate bar halves on tops of 12 graham cracker squares. Toast marshmallows over an open fire. Place toasted marshmallows on top of chocolate, and cover with remaining graham cracker squares to form a sandwich. Press to seal. Serve immediately. Yield: 6 servings.

Haul a few "easy-do" foods to the waterside, build just enough fire to toast wieners and marshmallows for S'Mores (wire coat hangers or green sticks will do for handles), and heat up the bean bake. Everything tastes good after a refreshing swim, even if the wieners and marshmallows char a bit.

Oyster-roast celebrants at Fort Marion in St. Augustine, Florida, 1905.

AT THE BEACH IN ST. AUGUSTINE

The March 10, 1900, issue of *The Tatler*, St. Augustine, Florida, reported "a very delightful day spent on the beach by a number of guests of the Magnolia [Hotel]. Among the pleasures was an oyster roast. . . . There is nothing more delicious in the world than the luscious bivalve when roasted in the shell just long enough to open it, and nowhere are they better than on the beach near here." This "bountiful repast" was given by a fashionable Pittsburgh woman who was wintering there. Indians taught the settlers to roast oysters, and we have not lost our taste for them, especially in the fall. How wonderfully simple! Put them on a grill, and roast until open.

ROASTED OYSTERS WITH
SPICY COCKTAIL SAUCE
GRILLED CORN
SLICED TOMATOES
CHARCOAL-BAKED POTATOES
ORANGE-GLAZED PECAN POUND CAKE
COLD BEER

Serves 4 to 6

ROASTED OYSTERS

4 to 6 dozen unshucked
 oysters
Spicy Cocktail Sauce

Scrub and rinse oysters thoroughly in cold water; drain.

Place 1 to 2 dozen oysters at a time on grill over medium-low coals; cover with a damp towel. Cover and cook 5 to 10 minutes or until shells begin to open.

Using an oyster knife, remove top shells, and sever oysters from half shells. Serve on half shells with Spicy Cocktail Sauce. Yield: 4 to 6 servings.

Spicy Cocktail Sauce:

½ cup catsup
½ cup chili sauce
1 tablespoon Worcestershire
 sauce
1 tablespoon prepared
 horseradish
1 teaspoon garlic salt
½ teaspoon dry
 mustard
⅛ teaspoon pepper

Combine all ingredients in a small bowl, stirring well. Chill. Yield: about 1 cup.

GRILLED CORN

½ cup butter or margarine,
 melted
1 teaspoon salt
½ teaspoon pepper
⅛ teaspoon red pepper
⅛ teaspoon garlic
 powder
6 ears fresh corn, husks and
 silks removed

Combine butter and seasonings in a small mixing bowl, mixing well. Brush corn with butter mixture.

Wrap each ear of corn in heavy-duty aluminum foil. Place corn on rack; cook over medium coals 45 minutes or until tender, turning frequently. Yield: 4 to 6 servings.

Serve Roasted Oysters with Cocktail Sauce, Baked Potatoes, Grilled Corn, and plenty of good, cold beer.

CHARCOAL-BAKED POTATOES

6 medium potatoes
Butter or sour cream
Salt and pepper to taste

Wrap each potato securely in heavy-duty aluminum foil. Place around grey coals on bottom of grill. Cook 1 hour and 15 minutes or until potatoes yield slightly to pressure. Turn potatoes every 20 minutes, using hot pads or tongs.

Unwrap potatoes, and cut a slit in top of each. Press sides to loosen inside of potato. Add butter or sour cream and seasonings to taste. Serve hot. Yield: 4 to 6 servings.

The kind of oyster roast given by the fashionable lady from Pittsburgh at the Magnolia and duly reported by the *St. Augustine Tatler* in 1900 has little in common with today's rollicking, informal party, except that it is still the luscious bivalve that brings us together. Hardwood fire is best for good, hot coals, and if you've no lid to put down over the oysters, just remember to cover them with wet burlap, and keep it wet.

Orange-Glazed Pecan Pound Cake (above) and 1890s trade card for fruit extracts company.

ORANGE-GLAZED PECAN POUND CAKE

1 cup butter
2½ cups sugar
6 eggs
2½ cups all-purpose flour, divided
1 cup finely chopped pecans
3 tablespoons self-rising flour
¼ teaspoon salt
1 cup milk
2 teaspoons vanilla extract
Orange Glaze
Grated orange zest

Cream butter; gradually add sugar, beating well. Add eggs, one at a time, beating well after each addition.

Combine ¼ cup all-purpose flour and pecans; stir to coat well, and set aside.

Sift together remaining flour and salt; add to creamed mixture alternately with milk, beginning and ending with flour mixture. Stir in pecans and vanilla. Pour into a greased and floured 10-inch tube pan. Bake at 325° for 1 hour and 20 minutes or until a wooden pick inserted near the center comes out clean.

Pour Orange Glaze evenly over hot cake. Garnish with orange zest. Cool in pan on a wire rack 15 minutes; remove from pan to cool completely. Yield: one 10-inch cake.

Orange Glaze:

⅔ cup sugar
¼ cup orange juice

Combine sugar and orange juice in a small saucepan; bring to a boil, stirring until sugar dissolves. Yield: glaze for one 10-inch cake.

BEACH PARTY ON SANTA ROSA ISLAND

anta Rosa Island, at the entrance to the harbor in Pensacola, has seen its share of picnics over the years. Back in 1899, it was being touted to prospective tourists and settlers as an oddity in our history: it is the site of Fort Pickens, the only Southern fort over which the Confederate flag never flew. Even in the 1890s, surf parties, with picnic baskets in tow, rode the trolley out to the beach, which provided bathhouses for the ladies and gentlemen. Dancing was a nightly pastime. Now part of the Gulf Islands National Seashore, Santa Rosa is still "the beach" to Pensacolans and the most perfect destination of all for well-provisioned picnickers and bathers.

CRISP OVEN-FRIED CHICKEN
PIMIENTO CHEESE SANDWICHES
PENSACOLA LAYERED SALAD
SUGAR COOKIES
WATERMELON

Serves 6 to 8

CRISP OVEN-FRIED CHICKEN

2 cups fine dry breadcrumbs
¾ cup grated Parmesan cheese
¼ cup chopped fresh parsley
2 teaspoons salt
½ teaspoon pepper
1 clove garlic, crushed
2 (3- to 3½-pound) broiler-fryers, cut up
1 cup butter or margarine, melted

Combine breadcrumbs, cheese, parsley, salt, pepper, and crushed garlic in a medium mixing bowl; mix well. Dip chicken, one piece at a time, in butter; dredge in crumb mixture. Arrange chicken pieces in a large aluminum foil-lined shallow baking pan. Bake, uncovered, at 350° for 1 hour or until chicken is tender, turning once. Drain on paper towels; serve warm or chilled. Yield: 6 to 8 servings.

A day in sun and surf, Santa Rosa Island. Ladies pose happily in an old beached skiff, 1908.

Fishing off the shores of Santa Rosa Island, c.1905.

SUGAR COOKIES

½ cup butter, softened
1 cup sugar
2 eggs
1 tablespoon whipping
   cream
1 tablespoon vanilla extract
2¼ cups all-purpose flour
1½ teaspoons baking
   powder
½ teaspoon salt
½ teaspoon ground nutmeg
Colored sugar

Cream butter in a large mixing bowl; gradually add 1 cup sugar, beating well. Add eggs, one at a time, beating well. Stir in whipping cream and vanilla.

Sift together flour, baking powder, salt, and nutmeg in a medium mixing bowl. Gradually add to creamed mixture, stirring well. Cover and chill.

Divide dough in half, keeping one half chilled until ready to use. Roll to ⅛-inch thickness on a well-floured surface; cut with assorted floured cookie cutters.

Place 1 inch apart on lightly greased cookie sheets. Sprinkle with colored sugar. Bake at 350° for 8 to 10 minutes. Remove from cookie sheets, and cool on wire racks. Repeat procedure with remaining dough. Yield: about 3 dozen.

PIMIENTO CHEESE SANDWICHES

½ (8-ounce) package cream
   cheese, softened
⅓ cup butter or margarine,
   softened
2 tablespoons mayonnaise
2 tablespoons minced
   pimiento
¼ teaspoon salt
¼ teaspoon paprika
16 slices thin-sliced whole
   wheat bread, crust removed

Combine cream cheese and butter; beat until smooth. Add remaining ingredients, except bread; mix until well blended.

Spread pimiento cheese mixture evenly over 8 bread slices. Top with remaining bread slices; cut in half crosswise. Yield: 8 sandwiches.

PENSACOLA LAYERED SALAD

3 medium cucumbers
4 medium tomatoes, sliced
   and quartered
2 green peppers, sliced,
   seeded, and quartered
2 cups mayonnaise
1 tablespoon olive oil
1 tablespoon vinegar
½ teaspoon Worcestershire
   sauce
1 clove garlic, minced
4 green onions, finely
   chopped
Paprika

Run a fork down side of cucumbers lengthwise, and cut into thin slices. Layer tomatoes, green peppers, and cucumbers in a large salad bowl.

Combine mayonnaise, oil, vinegar, Worcestershire sauce, and garlic; mix well. Spread over vegetables. Sprinkle with green onions and paprika. Cover and chill. Toss gently before serving; sprinkle with paprika. Yield: 6 to 8 servings.

Anyone visiting Pensacola at the turn of the century was entertained within an inch of his life. Fun was not limited to fair weather gambols on bay and bayou and the varied alfresco parties at the Pensacola Boat Club on the Bayou Chico. The dances and social clubs, busy with whist and euchre, also kept the party momentum going.

Beach fare: Pimiento Cheese Sandwiches, Pensacola Layered Salad, Watermelon.

FISHERMEN'S LAKESIDE SUPPER

The inland fisherman's idea of sport fishing more than likely means playing a fat bass from a boat in a freshwater lake or outfoxing a wily trout in a rushing stream. Once it was commonplace to find a "Closed, Gone Fishing" note hanging on the door of a small business during prime fishing weather. There are still fishermen serious enough to set aside time, put the makings of a shore-cooked meal in a cooler, and take off for a tried-and-true fishing hole. Catching an outsized bass or "cat" hiding out in a slew is a surefire way of getting one's picture in the paper. But first you must resist frying and eating it. Fish Stew is another palatable option.

FISH STEW
GARDEN SALAD WITH FRENCH DRESSING
CORNMEAL MUFFINS
QUICK BLACKBERRY COBBLER
or
FRESH BLACKBERRIES WITH CREAM

Serves 4 to 6

FISH STEW

2 slices bacon
2 tablespoons finely chopped onion
¾ pound freshwater fish fillets
¼ cup plus 2 tablespoons catsup
3½ cups water, divided
2 tablespoons all-purpose flour
⅔ cup instant non-fat dry milk powder
1 teaspoon salt

Cook bacon in a skillet until crisp; drain bacon, reserving drippings in skillet. Crumble bacon, and set aside.

Sauté onion in bacon drippings until tender; remove with a slotted spoon, and set aside.

Sauté fish in remaining drippings until fish is lightly browned. Remove fish from skillet, and cut into bite-size pieces. Combine bacon, onion, catsup, and ½ cup water in skillet. Simmer 5 minutes.

Combine flour, milk powder, salt, and remaining water in a medium saucepan, stirring well. Cook over medium heat, stirring constantly, until thickened. Stir in fish mixture. Cook until thoroughly heated. Yield: 5½ cups.

The makings for Quick Blackberry Cobbler and Fish Stew.

Preparing the catch after a day's fishing. c.1910.

GARDEN SALAD WITH FRENCH DRESSING

1 head iceberg lettuce
2 tomatoes, cut into wedges
1 cucumber, sliced
1¼ cups vegetable oil
1 teaspoon sugar
½ cup lemon juice
3 tablespoons chili sauce
1 teaspoon prepared
   horseradish
1 teaspoon prepared
   mustard
1 clove garlic, minced
1½ teaspoons salt
½ teaspoon paprika
¼ teaspoon pepper

Separate lettuce leaves. Wash thoroughly, and pat dry. Tear leaves into bite-size pieces. Combine lettuce, tomatoes, and cucumber in a serving bowl; toss lightly. Cover and chill thoroughly.

Combine oil, sugar, and lemon juice; beat with a wire whisk until well blended. Add remaining ingredients, mixing well. Chill thoroughly, and serve over tossed salad. Yield: 4 to 6 servings.

CORNMEAL MUFFINS

1 cup cornmeal
1 cup all-purpose flour
½ cup instant non-fat dry
   milk powder
1 tablespoon baking powder
1 teaspoon salt
1½ cups water
2 eggs, beaten
¼ cup shortening, melted

Combine cornmeal, flour, milk, baking powder, and salt in a medium mixing bowl; stir well. Combine remaining ingredients; add to cornmeal mixture, mixing just until dry ingredients are moistened.

Spoon batter into greased muffin pans, filling two-thirds full. Bake at 425° for 20 minutes or until golden brown. Yield: 1½ dozen.

QUICK BLACKBERRY COBBLER

¼ cup plus 2 tablespoons
   butter or margarine
1½ cups sugar, divided
¾ cup all-purpose flour
2 teaspoons baking powder
Dash of salt
¾ cup milk
2 cups fresh blackberries

Melt butter in a 2-quart baking dish.

Combine 1 cup sugar, flour, baking powder, and salt in a large mixing bowl. Add milk; stir well. Pour batter over butter in baking dish. Do not stir.

Combine blackberries and remaining sugar; spoon over batter. Do not stir. Bake at 350° for 1 hour or until crust is browned. Yield: 4 to 6 servings.

GAME FISH CELEBRATION IN PENSACOLA

More and more sport fishermen who go for the big billfish out of Pensacola and other Gulf ports have learned that the marlin, unlike the tarpon, is a desirable food fish. Blue or white marlins average three hundred to four hundred pounds, though they may grow much larger, and resemble the swordfish, to which they are not related. In this country, marlins are considered game fish only, illegal to buy or sell. However, many are discovering its value as table fare. In Japan, marlin is prized for making sashimi and fish sausage. Marlin steaks certainly compete with t-bones; they are excellent for smoking, and they freeze well.

MARLIN CHOWDER
WHITE MARLIN GUMBO
HOT COOKED RICE
BARBECUED MARLIN
FRIED MARLIN NUGGETS
SUMMER SLAW
SOUR CREAM POTATO SALAD
CHEWY BROWNIES
BEER

Serves 12

MARLIN CHOWDER

4 onions, chopped
4 stalks celery, chopped
2 green peppers, seeded and chopped
4 cloves garlic, crushed
¼ cup vegetable oil
4 (14½-ounce) cans tomatoes, undrained and chopped
1 quart water
6 potatoes, peeled and cubed
¼ cup Worcestershire sauce
3 tablespoons lemon juice
2 teaspoons salt
1 teaspoon ground cloves
½ teaspoon ground allspice
½ teaspoon hot sauce
2 pounds marlin fillets, cut into bite-size pieces

Sauté onion, celery, green pepper, and crushed garlic in oil in a large Dutch oven until tender. Add tomatoes; simmer, uncovered, 40 minutes, stirring occasionally.

Add remaining ingredients, except fish; simmer 1 hour or until potatoes are tender. Add fish; simmer 5 minutes or until fish flakes easily when tested with a fork. Yield: 5 quarts

WHITE MARLIN GUMBO

2 slices bacon
2 medium onions, chopped
3 stalks celery, chopped
¼ cup vegetable oil
¼ cup all-purpose flour
1½ quarts water
1 (16-ounce) can tomatoes, drained and chopped
1½ cups sliced okra
1 (8-ounce) can tomato sauce
2 tablespoons lemon juice
1 teaspoon celery salt
½ teaspoon salt
½ teaspoon pepper
½ teaspoon minced garlic
Dash of hot sauce
1 pound medium shrimp, peeled and deveined
1½ pounds marlin fillets, cut into bite-size pieces
Hot cooked rice

Cook bacon in a heavy skillet until crisp; remove bacon, reserving drippings in skillet. Drain bacon on a paper towel; crumble and set aside.

Sauté onion and celery in drippings until tender; set aside.

Combine oil and flour in a large stockpot, stirring until smooth. Cook over medium heat, stirring occasionally, until roux is the color of a copper penny. Stir in sautéed vegetables, water, tomatoes, okra, tomato sauce, lemon juice, celery salt, salt, pepper, garlic, and hot sauce; cook over low heat 45 minutes, stirring occasionally.

Stir in shrimp and marlin; cook an additional 10 minutes or until shrimp are pink and firm. Serve gumbo immediately over hot cooked rice. Yield: about 3 quarts.

Summer Slaw (rear) with Barbecued Marlin on skewers and Marlin Chowder: reason enough to celebrate the catch.

BARBECUED MARLIN

4 pounds white marlin, cut
  into 1-inch cubes
½ cup Worcestershire sauce
½ cup teriyaki sauce
½ cup butter or margarine,
  melted
½ cup lemon juice
2 teaspoons curry powder
1 teaspoon pepper
Fresh parsley sprigs

Place marlin in a large mixing
bowl. Combine remaining ingredients, except parsley; mix
well. Pour over marlin; stir well.
Cover and refrigerate 1 hour.
Stir mixture occasionally. Drain
marlin; reserve marinade.

Thread marlin onto skewers.
Place skewers on rack 5 or 6
inches over medium coals. Grill
until fish flakes easily when
tested with a fork, basting frequently with marinade.

Transfer marlin to a warm
serving platter; garnish with
parsley. Serve on wooden picks.
Yield: 12 appetizer servings.

FRIED MARLIN NUGGETS

4 pounds marlin fillets, cut
  into 1½-inch cubes
2 cups buttermilk
3 cups cornmeal
1 cup all-purpose flour
2 teaspoons salt
2 teaspoons pepper
2 teaspoons celery salt
2 teaspoons onion salt
Peanut oil
Commercial cocktail sauce
  (optional)

Soak marlin cubes in buttermilk in a shallow baking dish 30
minutes.

Combine cornmeal, flour,
salt, and seasonings in a plastic
or paper bag; shake to mix well.
Place several marlin cubes in
bag; shake well. Drop coated
marlin into deep, hot oil (375°).
Fry 5 minutes or until golden
brown. Drain well. Repeat procedure with remaining marlin.
Serve with cocktail sauce, if desired. Yield: 12 servings.

*Around 1895, one could
mosey down to the wharf
at St. Petersburg, wet a line,
and take home a nice fish.*

SUMMER SLAW

12 cups chopped cabbage
  (about 2 medium cabbages)
3 medium onions, coarsely
  chopped
3 medium tomatoes, peeled
  and chopped
¾ cup sugar
½ cup tomato juice
¼ cup vinegar
2½ teaspoons salt
¾ teaspoon pepper
Onion rings (optional)

Combine cabbage, onion, and
tomato in a large mixing bowl.
Set aside.

Combine sugar, tomato juice,
vinegar, salt, and pepper; mix
well. Pour over cabbage mixture; toss. Cover and chill.

Garnish with onion rings before serving, if desired. Yield: 12
servings.

SOUR CREAM POTATO SALAD

10 medium potatoes (about
    3½ pounds)
9 slices bacon, cooked and
    crumbled
3 hard-cooked eggs, chopped
1 medium onion, minced
¾ cup chopped sweet pickle
3 tablespoons sweet pickle
    juice
1½ cups commercial sour
    cream
3 tablespoons cider vinegar
1 tablespoon prepared
    mustard
1½ teaspoons salt
½ teaspoon pepper
Lettuce leaves
1 hard-cooked egg, sliced

Cook potatoes in boiling salted water 25 minutes or until potatoes are tender. Drain well, and cool slightly. Peel potatoes, and cut in half lengthwise. Cut each half into ¼-inch-thick slices crosswise.

Combine sliced potatoes, bacon, chopped eggs, onion, pickle, pickle juice, sour cream, vinegar, mustard, salt, and pepper in a large bowl; toss gently until well blended. Spoon mixture into a lettuce-lined bowl; garnish with sliced egg. Cover and refrigerate until ready to serve. Yield: 12 servings.

I n the early 1900s, English Historian Oscar Browning came to Savannah to visit Juliet Gordon Low and her parents. Her husband took him on a chartered train to Florida to "still fish" for tarpon. In his *Memories of Sixty Years*, he relates that his first catch was a hammerhead. Using heavy whipcord line and an African kingwood reel, he brought up a somersaulting tarpon and fully understood the thrill of game fishing.

CHEWY BROWNIES

1 cup butter or margarine
4 (1-ounce) squares
    unsweetened chocolate
4 eggs
2 cups sugar
1½ cups all-purpose flour
½ teaspoon baking powder
1 cup chopped pecans
1 teaspoon vanilla extract
2¼ cups sifted powdered
    sugar
½ cup chocolate-flavored
    syrup

Melt butter and chocolate squares in top of a double boiler over simmering water; set mixture aside to cool.

Combine eggs and 2 cups sugar; mix well. Combine flour and baking powder; mix well. Add to egg mixture, stirring well. Stir in chocolate mixture, pecans, and vanilla; mix well. Pour into a greased 13- x 9- x 2-inch baking pan. Bake at 325° for 35 minutes.

Combine powdered sugar and syrup; spread over warm brownies. Cool completely in pan before cutting into 2-inch squares. Yield: about 2 dozen.

Small fry, big catch, 1905.

Collection of Linda Campbell Franklin

ON THE GREEN

MENU OF MENUS

AFTERNOON LAWN PARTY

TENNIS CHAMPIONSHIP
PARTY

BRUNCH BEFORE THE
MASTERS

GOLF TEA AT JEKYLL
ISLAND

FOOTBALL TAILGATE
PICNIC

TEXAS-OKLAHOMA
WEEKEND PARTY

SUGAR BOWL FARE AT
BUSTER HOLMES

SCOTTISH HIGHLAND
GAMES PICNIC

*A sumptuous lawn-party
meal ends on a dainty
note in this serene setting:
Glazed Fruit Tarts
complement Champagne
Punch. A sure cure
for sticky wickets.*

Sports performed on the green are as diverse as the kinds of surfaces that make up modern-day green-swards. Multitudes of Southerners make yearly pilgrimages in the name of tennis, golf, and football. Croquet is a comer, and vacationers in mid-July watch antiquated Scottish games on Grandfather Mountain in North Carolina. Parties before or after the games are a given, but in selecting the menu, again, we have diversity—a tailgate picnic or an opulent Victorian-style lawn party.

Since 1977 when the United States Croquet Association was formed, 220 croquet clubs have sprung up. The nationally sanctioned croquet tournament is played on a rolled 84-x 105-foot greensward with six cast-iron hoops, barely wide enough for the standardized one-pound Eclispe ball to pass through. That's croquet today, but when it came to America in the 1870s, it was perfectly suited to the wide lawns of Southern estates. The croquet party luncheon was as expansive as the estate on which the game was played, the sort of menu offered here.

How folks do turn out when a famous tennis player comes in town for a tournament! The world's darlings among tennis champions have "personalities" such as only some stage and movie star *enfants terribles* once dared exhibit, but it only adds to their drawing power.

American golfing greats are among our most adored athletes, and their "galleries" of followers, for whom no trip is too long, reserve the first week of April for the Masters Tournament in Augusta, Georgia.

The South goes all out for its football heroes, too. The Sugar Bowl, Orange Bowl, Cotton Bowl—are of national importance. But the partisanship engendered by ancient rivalries between colleges in the South brings out even more zealous followings. Tennessee-Kentucky, Texas-Oklahoma, Auburn-Alabama—there are many such "archenemy" athletic clubs. Tailgate lunches have become the out-of-town fans' best pre-game spirit raiser. The popular restaurants in town will be packed with players and fans. Buster Holmes historic New Orleans restaurant is one such.

The Gathering of Scottish Clans in this chapter wraps up the most tempting of Southern playtime menus.

AFTERNOON LAWN PARTY

Before we write off croquet as a non-sport with neither history nor an active following, consider that in sixteenth-century France, kings played it as *paille maille* (ball and mallet). In the 1700s, royalty and upper-class Englishmen played it as "crookery," named for the shepherds' crooks used for clubs. And lest we think croquet a grassy form of shuffleboard for the elderly or a rarified kind of outdoor chess for the smart set, this news: 220 croquet clubs have sprung up since 1977. There are four sanctioned clubs in North Carolina alone, three in Virginia. For a croquet party: an opulent Victorian-style menu with lobster dishes and champagne.

BROILED OYSTERS
LOBSTER NEWBURG IN PATTY SHELLS
LOBSTER-STUFFED EGGS
TOMATOES STUFFED WITH MUSHROOMS
VEGETABLE SALAD MOLD
PICKLES * OLIVES
GLAZED FRUIT TARTS
CHAMPAGNE PUNCH

Serves 8 to 10

BROILED OYSTERS

1 cup cracker crumbs
  (buttery round crackers)
1 (12-ounce) container Select
  oysters, drained
¼ cup butter
¼ cup water
2 tablespoons Worcestershire
  sauce
1 lemon, sliced
1 teaspoon pepper

Sprinkle cracker crumbs evenly in 10 crab shells or ramekins. Place 2 or 3 oysters over cracker crumbs in each shell. Melt butter in a small saucepan over low heat; add remaining ingredients, and cook until thoroughly heated. Remove and discard lemon.

Drizzle 2 teaspoons butter mixture evenly over oysters in shells. Place shells on a broiling pan, and broil 5 inches from heating element 5 minutes. Serve immediately. Yield: 8 to 10 appetizer servings.

Croquet on the lawn of a Virginia home near Rockbridge, circa 1870.

LOBSTER NEWBURG IN PATTY SHELLS

¼ cup plus 2 tablespoons butter or margarine
3 tablespoons all-purpose flour
1½ cups whipping cream
¼ teaspoon salt
¾ teaspoon paprika
¼ teaspoon ground nutmeg
4 egg yolks, beaten
3 cups chopped, cooked lobster
3 tablespoons sherry
10 baked commercial patty shells

Melt butter in top of a double boiler over simmering water; add flour, stirring until smooth. Cook 1 minute, stirring constantly. Gradually add whipping cream; cook over boiling water, stirring constantly, until mixture thickens. Stir in salt, paprika, and nutmeg.

Stir a small amount of hot mixture into yolks; return yolk mixture to remaining hot mixture. Continue to cook over boiling water until mixture is thickened and bubbly. Stir in lobster and sherry. Spoon evenly into patty shells. Yield: 10 servings.

LOBSTER-STUFFED EGGS

½ pound finely chopped, cooked lobster
⅔ cup mayonnaise
1 tablespoon chili sauce
1 teaspoon grated onion
1 teaspoon chopped green pepper
1 teaspoon chopped pimiento
12 hard-cooked eggs
Fresh parsley leaves

Combine lobster, mayonnaise, chili sauce, onion, green pepper, and pimiento; stir well. Cover and chill.

Slice eggs in half lengthwise, and remove yolks. Mash yolks, and add to chilled mixture, stirring well. Stuff whites with lobster mixture. Garnish each stuffed egg with a parsley leaf. Yield: 8 to 10 servings.

Featuring: lobster in Newburg and eggs; mushrooms in tomatoes.

TOMATOES STUFFED WITH MUSHROOMS

10 small tomatoes
1½ pounds fresh mushrooms, sliced
3 tablespoons butter or margarine
¾ cup commercial sour cream
¾ teaspoon salt
¼ teaspoon pepper
9 slices bacon, cooked and crumbled
Chopped fresh chives

Remove stems, and cut a ¼-inch slice from the top of each tomato. Scoop out pulp, leaving shells intact; reserve pulp for other uses. Invert tomato shells onto paper towels to drain; set aside.

Sauté mushrooms in butter in a large skillet until tender. Remove from heat, and gradually stir in sour cream, salt, and pepper.

Spoon mixture into prepared tomato shells; sprinkle bacon on top of each. Place tomatoes in a lightly greased 15- x 10- x 1-inch jellyroll pan. Bake at 350° for 15 to 20 minutes. Garnish with chives; serve warm. Yield: 10 servings.

VEGETABLE SALAD MOLD

2 envelopes unflavored gelatin
1 cup cold water
¼ cup lemon juice
1 teaspoon salt
½ teaspoon hot sauce
1½ cups mayonnaise or salad dressing
1 cup finely chopped celery
1 cup finely chopped green pepper
1 (4-ounce) jar sliced pimiento, drained
1 tablespoon grated onion
Leaf lettuce
4 hard-cooked eggs, sliced

Soften gelatin in cold water in top of a double boiler. Cook over boiling water, stirring constantly, until gelatin dissolves. Remove from heat; add lemon juice, salt, and hot sauce. Cool. Chill to consistency of unbeaten egg white. Stir in mayonnaise, celery, green pepper, pimiento, and onion. Pour mixture into a lightly oiled 4-cup mold; chill until firm.

Unmold salad onto a lettuce-lined serving plate. Garnish with egg slices. Yield: 8 to 10 servings.

GLAZED FRUIT TARTS

¼ cup sugar
1 tablespoon cornstarch
⅓ cup orange juice
3 tablespoons cold water
1 cup seedless grapes
¾ cup sliced, peeled
  peaches
½ cup sliced fresh
  strawberries
½ cup fresh blueberries
1 small banana, peeled and
  sliced
Tart Shells

Combine sugar, cornstarch, orange juice, and water in a small saucepan. Cook over medium heat, stirring constantly, until mixture is thickened and clear. Set aside to cool.

Arrange grapes, peaches, strawberries, blueberries, and banana, as desired, in tart shells. Spoon orange mixture evenly over fruit in tart shells. Yield: 12 tarts.

Tart Shells:

1½ cups all-purpose flour
¼ teaspoon salt
3 tablespoons shortening
3 tablespoons cold
  water

Combine flour and salt in a small mixing bowl; cut in shortening with a pastry blender until mixture resembles coarse meal. Sprinkle water evenly over surface of flour mixture; stir with a fork just until dry ingredients are moistened.

Divide dough into 16 equal balls. Place each ball in an ungreased 4-inch tart pan; press dough into pans to form shells. Prick bottom of each shell several times with a fork. Place tart pan on a baking sheet; bake at 475° for 10 minutes or until lightly browned. Cool completely in pans. Yield: 16 tarts shells.

Note: Extra tart shells may be frozen for other uses.

Two can play at an intimate croquet game, c.1910.

CHAMPAGNE PUNCH

3 (750 ml) bottles club soda,
  divided
2 cups water
1 lemon, sliced and seeded
12 maraschino cherries
Peeled rind and juice of 2
  lemons
3 cups sugar
4 (25.4-ounce) bottles
  champagne, chilled
1 (750 ml) bottle Rhine wine
2 cups sherry

Combine 1 bottle club soda and water, stirring well.

Arrange lemon slices and cherries in a 6-cup ring mold; gently pour 1 cup club soda mixture into mold; freeze. Pour remaining club soda mixture over frozen mold; freeze until ready to use.

Combine lemon rind and juice, sugar, and 2 bottles club soda, stirring well. Let stand 1 hour, stirring frequently. Remove rind, and discard.

Unmold ice ring in a punch bowl. Gently pour lemon mixture, champagne, wine, and sherry over ring. Serve immediately. Yield: 8 to 10 servings.

TENNIS CHAMPIONSHIP PARTY

King George III adored tennis, but the game he played is now called court tennis or real tennis. The modern version is considered a mere fad by a few diehards. French monks began the sport in the Middle Ages. In the cities, it was played on walled-in courts to simulate the cloister. Royalty sometimes went overboard for tennis: Charles IX of France spent six hours a day "on the green." Championship tennis, over the years, has enjoyed an immense following. Newport Casino, Rhode Island, hosted the first U.S. National Championship in 1881. R. D. Sears, the winner, remained U.S. Champion until 1888. Here's a party for after the match. You serve!

COLD CUCUMBER SOUP
SPINACH MOLD
DILL SHRIMP
STEAMED FRESH ASPARAGUS
PINEAPPLE-MINT GLAZED LAMB
SAVORY STUFFED SQUASH
LEMON PARFAIT
FRENCH LACE COOKIES
WINE SPRITZERS
ICED TEA

Serves 8

Pineapple-Mint Glazed Lamb, steamed fresh asparagus, Stuffed Squash.

This Cold Cucumber Soup is surprisingly rich and creamy. A perfect first course for a summer party.

COLD CUCUMBER SOUP

2 large cucumbers, peeled, seeded, and coarsely grated
2 cups whipping cream
1 cup plain yogurt
¼ cup tarragon vinegar
1 clove garlic, crushed
½ teaspoon salt
⅛ teaspoon white pepper
Cucumber slices

Combine all ingredients, except cucumber slices; stir well. Chill. Ladle into individual bowls. Garnish with cucumber slices. Yield: 1 quart.

SPINACH MOLD

1 envelope unflavored gelatin
¼ cup cold water
1 (10-ounce) package frozen chopped spinach
½ cup mayonnaise
1 tablespoon prepared horseradish
2 teaspoons minced onion
2 teaspoons lemon juice
½ teaspoon salt
½ teaspoon pepper
⅛ teaspoon hot sauce
½ cup commercial sour cream
Assorted crackers

Soften gelatin in water in top of a double boiler 5 minutes; cook over simmering water, stirring until gelatin dissolves.

Cook spinach according to package directions, omitting salt; drain well.

Combine dissolved gelatin, spinach, mayonnaise, horseradish, onion, lemon juice, salt, pepper, and hot sauce in container of an electric blender; process until smooth.

Spoon mixture into a lightly oiled 1½-cup mold or bowl. Chill overnight. Unmold onto a serving platter. Spread sour cream over mold. Serve with crackers. Yield: 8 appetizer servings.

DILL SHRIMP

2 cups water
1½ teaspoons salt
½ teaspoon dried whole dillweed
1 lemon, sliced
1¼ pounds uncooked medium shrimp
Dill Marinade
2 medium cucumbers, thinly sliced

Combine first 4 ingredients in a medium saucepan; bring to a boil. Add shrimp; simmer 3 minutes or until pink. Drain; peel and devein shrimp. Pour Dill Marinade over shrimp; cover and refrigerate 24 hours.

Drain shrimp, discarding marinade. Secure each shrimp to a cucumber slice, using a wooden pick. Yield: 8 servings.

Dill Marinade:

½ cup olive oil
½ cup Chablis or other dry white wine
½ cup lemon juice
1 tablespoon plus 1 teaspoon dried whole dillweed
1 tablespoon chopped green onion tops
1 teaspoon garlic powder
1 teaspoon salt
1 teaspoon pepper
⅛ teaspoon hot sauce

Combine all ingredients in a small bowl; mix well. Yield: about 1½ cups.

PINEAPPLE-MINT GLAZED LAMB

½ cup olive oil
¼ cup vinegar
¼ cup dry sherry
2 cloves garlic, crushed
2 teaspoons dried mint flakes
2 teaspoons salt
2 teaspoons pepper
1 (5- to 6-pound) leg of lamb
1 (10-ounce) jar mint-flavored apple jelly
1 (8¼-ounce) can crushed pineapple, undrained

Combine first 7 ingredients in a small mixing bowl, and mix until well blended.

Remove the fell (tissue-like covering) from roast with a sharp knife. Place roast in a 15- x 10- x 1-inch jellyroll pan; pour marinade over roast. Marinate 2 hours, turning roast every 30 minutes.

Line a shallow roasting pan with aluminum foil; lightly grease rack of roasting pan. Place roast, fat side up, on rack. Insert meat thermometer, if desired, being careful not to touch bone or fat.

Combine jelly and pineapple in a small saucepan. Cook over low heat until jelly dissolves. Baste roast frequently with jelly mixture. Bake at 350° until desired degree of doneness: about 1½ hours or 140° (rare); about 2½ hours or 160° (medium); about 3 hours or 170° (well done).

Transfer roast to a serving platter. Cool slightly. Garnish as desired. Yield: 8 servings.

Tennis fashions have changed since 1905, when these young ladies played.

Taking a break from the courts, players relax in and under a tree, 1886.

SAVORY STUFFED SQUASH

8 medium-size yellow squash
2 small onions, chopped
3 small carrots, shredded
¼ cup butter or margarine, divided
1 (2-ounce) jar sliced pimiento, drained
2 cups herb-seasoned stuffing mix, divided
½ cup commercial sour cream
½ teaspoon salt
¼ teaspoon pepper

Place squash in a saucepan with boiling water to cover. Cook over medium heat 10 minutes or until tender. Drain; cool.

Cut a ¼-inch lengthwise slice from each squash; scoop out, and reserve pulp, leaving shells intact. Mash pulp, and set aside. Remove ends of squash.

Sauté reserved pulp, onion, and carrots in 1 tablespoon butter in a large skillet until tender. Remove from heat; stir in pimiento, 1 cup stuffing mix, sour cream, salt, and pepper. Spoon mixture into shells.

Place stuffed squash in a lightly greased 13- x 9- x 2-inch baking dish. Combine remaining stuffing mix with remaining butter; sprinkle evenly over each squash. Bake at 400° for 10 minutes or until thoroughly heated. Yield: 8 servings.

LEMON PARFAIT

2 envelopes unflavored gelatin
½ cup cold water
4 eggs, separated
½ cup fresh lemon juice
1 cup sugar, divided
¼ teaspoon salt
2 teaspoons grated lemon rind
1 teaspoon lemon extract
1 cup whipping cream
1 teaspoon vanilla extract
8 thin slices lemon

Soften gelatin in cold water 5 minutes.

Combine egg yolks, lemon juice, ½ cup sugar, and salt in top of a double boiler. Cook over boiling water, stirring constantly, until thickened. Add softened gelatin, lemon rind, and lemon extract; stir well. Continue to cook over boiling water, stirring until gelatin dissolves. Cool completely. Transfer to a large mixing bowl.

Beat egg whites (at room temperature) until foamy. Gradually add remaining sugar, 1 tablespoon at a time, beating until stiff peaks form. Gently fold into lemon mixture.

Beat whipping cream and vanilla until soft peaks form. Fold into lemon mixture. Spoon evenly into parfait glasses; cover and chill. Garnish with lemon slices. Yield: 8 servings.

FRENCH LACE COOKIES

1 cup all-purpose flour
1 cup finely chopped pecans
⅔ cup firmly packed brown sugar
½ cup light corn syrup
½ cup butter or margarine

Combine flour and pecans in a medium mixing bowl, stirring well. Set aside.

Combine sugar, syrup, and butter in a small saucepan. Cook over medium heat just to boiling, stirring occasionally. Remove from heat; add to flour mixture, stirring well.

Drop batter by teaspoonfuls 3 inches apart onto aluminum foil-lined cookie sheets. Bake at 350° for 7 minutes. Let cool completely on cookie sheets; peel off aluminum foil. Store cookies in airtight containers. Yield: 4 dozen.

WINE SPRITZERS

1 (28-ounce) bottle club soda, chilled
1 (750-ml) bottle Rhine wine

Combine club soda and wine; pour over ice in glasses. Yield: 2 quarts.

BRUNCH BEFORE THE MASTERS

During the first week in April, the golfing world comes into focus at the Augusta National Golf Club, Augusta, Georgia. The golf enthusiast cannot attend the Masters Tournament without an overwhelming reverence for the environs hallowed by the great sportsman who helped make the Masters happen—Bobby Jones.

Bobby had accomplished the impossible "grand slam," winning the Open and Amateur championships of Great Britain and the U.S. in the same year, 1930. He remained the spirit of the Masters until his health failed in 1948. Who'll be next to wear the green coat of the champion? It will be decided in hospitable Augusta next April.

BLOODY BULLS
EGG CASSEROLE
CHEESE PUFFS
CARROT SOUFFLÉ
BOURBON-GLAZED HAM
EMERALD SALAD
ZUCCHINI BREAD
SOUR FRENCH BREAD
WINE BARS
ICE CREAM CAKE

Serves 12

BLOODY BULLS

2 (46-ounce) cans tomato
  juice
2 (10½-ounce) cans beef
  broth, undiluted
2 cups vodka
¼ cup lemon
  juice
2 tablespoons lime juice
2 tablespoons Worcestershire
  sauce
2 teaspoons salt
½ teaspoon
  pepper
½ teaspoon hot sauce
⅛ teaspoon celery
  seeds
Lemon or lime twists

Combine all ingredients, except lemon or lime twists; stir well, and chill mixture thoroughly. To serve, pour mixture over ice in glasses. Garnish with lemon or lime twists. Yield: about 1 gallon.

Guests will relax happily over peppery Bloody Bulls while the Egg Casserole finishes baking in the oven.

EGG CASSEROLE

¼ cup butter or margarine
¼ cup all-purpose flour
1 cup milk
1 cup half-and-half
1 pound sharp Cheddar
  cheese, shredded
¼ cup chopped fresh
  parsley
¼ teaspoon dried whole
  thyme
¼ teaspoon dried whole basil
¼ teaspoon salt
⅛ teaspoon pepper
1 clove garlic, crushed
18 hard-cooked eggs, sliced
12 slices bacon, cooked and
  crumbled
3 cups soft breadcrumbs
¼ cup plus 2 tablespoons
  butter or margarine, melted

Melt ¼ cup butter in a heavy saucepan over low heat; add flour, stirring until smooth. Cook 1 minute, stirring constantly. Gradually add milk and half-and-half; cook over medium heat, stirring until thickened and bubbly. Add cheese, stirring until cheese melts. Stir in seasonings and garlic.

Spread one-third of sauce in bottom of a greased 13- x 9- x 2-inch baking dish. Layer half of sliced eggs and half of crumbled bacon over sauce. Repeat layers, ending with sauce.

Combine breadcrumbs and melted butter; sprinkle over casserole. Bake at 350° for 25 minutes or until bubbly and browned. Serve hot. Yield: 12 servings.

CHEESE PUFFS

2 cups all-purpose flour
1 tablespoon baking powder
½ teaspoon salt
½ teaspoon red pepper
2 cups (8 ounces) shredded
  sharp Cheddar cheese
2 eggs
1½ cups milk
½ cup vegetable oil

Sift together flour, baking powder, salt, and pepper; add cheese, mixing well.

Combine eggs, milk, and oil; mix well. Pour over top of cheese mixture, stirring just until dry ingredients are moistened.

Spoon mixture into greased miniature muffin pans, filling two-thirds full. Bake at 425° for 10 minutes or until lightly browned. Yield: 3 dozen.

CARROT SOUFFLÉ

2 pounds carrots, scraped,
  cooked, and pureed
¼ cup plus 2 tablespoons
  butter or margarine
¼ cup plus 2 tablespoons
  all-purpose flour
2 cups milk
6 eggs
¼ cup plus 2 tablespoons
  sugar
1 teaspoon ground nutmeg
½ teaspoon salt
2 teaspoons vanilla extract

Set pureed carrots aside in a large mixing bowl to cool.

Melt butter in a heavy saucepan over low heat; add flour, stirring until smooth. Cook 1 minute, stirring constantly. Gradually add milk; cook over medium heat, stirring constantly, until mixture is thickened and bubbly.

Beat eggs in a small mixing bowl; gradually stir in one-fourth of hot white sauce. Add egg mixture to remaining white sauce, stirring constantly. Remove from heat. Add white sauce, sugar, nutmeg, salt, and vanilla to reserved carrots; mix well. Spoon mixture into a 2-quart soufflé dish. Bake at 350° for 1 hour and 25 minutes. Remove from oven, and let stand 5 minutes before serving. Yield: 12 servings.

BOURBON-GLAZED HAM

1 (7- to 8-pound) fully cooked
  butt portion ham
1 cup bourbon
1 cup firmly packed brown
  sugar
1 teaspoon grated orange rind
¼ teaspoon ground cloves
25 whole cloves

Place ham in a shallow baking pan, fat side up. Bake, uncovered, at 325° for 1½ hours.

Combine bourbon, sugar, orange rind, and ground cloves in a small mixing bowl, stirring well; let stand 30 minutes, stirring frequently to dissolve sugar.

Remove outer layer of skin from ham. Score fat in a diamond pattern, and stud with whole cloves.

Baste ham with bourbon mixture. Return ham to oven, and bake, uncovered, at 350° for 1 hour, basting frequently with bourbon mixture.

Transfer ham to a serving platter; cool slightly before slicing. Yield: 12 servings.
Note: Cover and store leftover ham in refrigerator.

*Emerald Salad (front).
Clockwise: Carrot Soufflé,
Sour French Bread, and
Bourbon-Glazed Ham.*

EMERALD SALAD

1 (3-ounce) package
  lime-flavored gelatin
¼ cup cold water
½ cup boiling water
1 cup cottage cheese
1 cup mayonnaise
¾ cup shredded cucumber
⅓ cup slivered almonds,
  toasted
2 tablespoons grated onion
Lettuce leaves
Additional mayonnaise
Additional slivered almonds,
  toasted

Soften gelatin in cold water 5 minutes; add to boiling water, stirring until gelatin dissolves. Chill until mixture reaches the consistency of unbeaten egg white. Gently fold in remaining ingredients, except lettuce leaves, additional mayonnaise, and additional almonds. Spoon mixture into a lightly-oiled 4-cup mold. Chill until firm.

Unmold salad onto a chilled, lettuce-lined plate. Dollop with mayonnaise, and sprinkle with additional almonds. Yield: 12 servings.

ZUCCHINI BREAD

4 eggs, well beaten
1½ cups sugar
1 cup vegetable oil
3½ cups all-purpose flour
¾ teaspoon baking powder
1½ teaspoons baking soda
1½ teaspoons salt
1 teaspoon ground
  cinnamon
2 cups grated zucchini
1 cup chopped pecans
1 teaspoon vanilla extract

Combine eggs, sugar, and oil; beat well. Sift together dry ingredients; add to egg mixture, stirring until blended. Stir in zucchini, pecans, and vanilla; mix well.

Pour batter into 2 greased 8½- x 4½- x 3-inch loafpans. Bake 1 hour and 10 minutes or until a wooden pick inserted in center comes out clean. Cool 10 minutes, and remove from pans; cool completely. Yield: 2 loaves.

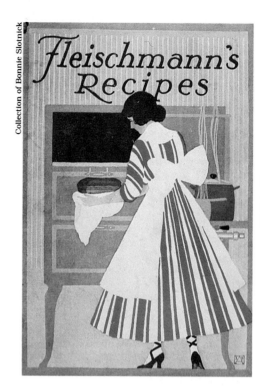

Cover of 1915 recipe booklet.

SOUR FRENCH BREAD

2 packages dry yeast
2 tablespoons sugar
4½ cups all-purpose
  flour, divided
1 (12-ounce) can flat beer,
  divided
½ cup milk
1½ cups whole wheat flour
2 teaspoons salt
¼ cup vegetable oil
Additional whole wheat flour

Combine yeast, sugar, and 1 cup all-purpose flour in a large mixing bowl; mix well. Heat ¾ cup beer to 120° to 130°; add to dry ingredients, stirring well. Cover and let rise in a warm place (85°), free from drafts, 20 minutes or until spongy and doubled in bulk.

Scald milk; let cool to lukewarm (105° to 115°). Heat remaining beer to 105° to 115°. Stir yeast mixture down; add milk, beer, 1½ cups whole wheat flour, salt, and oil, stirring well. Gradually add remaining all-purpose flour, stirring until dough leaves sides of bowl. Turn dough out onto a lightly floured surface, and knead 5

minutes or until dough is smooth and elastic. Place dough in a greased bowl, turning to grease top. Cover and repeat rising procedure 1 hour or until doubled in bulk.

Punch dough down. Turn dough out onto a lightly floured surface; knead 5 minutes or until dough is smooth and elastic. Place dough in a greased bowl, turning to grease top. Cover and repeat rising procedure 50 minutes or until doubled in bulk.

Punch dough down. Turn dough out onto a lightly floured surface; knead 5 minutes or until smooth and elastic. Divide in half; knead each half 3 minutes. Shape halves into balls. Place into 2 greased 8-inch round cakepans. Sprinkle tops with additional whole wheat flour. Cover and repeat rising procedure 45 minutes or until doubled in bulk.

Bake at 450° for 20 to 25 minutes or until loaves sound hollow when tapped. Remove bread from pans immediately; cool on wire racks. Yield: 2 loaves.

WINE BARS

1 cup butter or margarine
1½ cups firmly packed brown
    sugar
2 eggs
1 cup all-purpose flour
1 teaspoon baking powder
¼ cup port wine
¼ cup milk
2 cups finely chopped pecans
    or walnuts
1 tablespoon vanilla
    extract
Glaze (recipe follows)

Cream butter; gradually add sugar, beating until light and fluffy. Add eggs, beating well.

Combine flour and baking powder; add to creamed mixture alternately with wine and milk, beginning and ending with flour mixture. Stir in pecans and vanilla. Pour batter into a greased and floured 13- x 9- x 2-inch baking pan.

Bake at 350° for 25 minutes or until a wooden pick inserted in center comes out clean. Remove from oven; cool completely in pan on a wire rack. Pour glaze over cake; chill before cutting into 3- x 2-inch bars. Yield: about 1½ dozen.

Glaze:

2 tablespoons butter or
    margarine, softened
2 cups sifted powdered sugar
3 tablespoons port wine
Dash of salt

Cream butter. Gradually add sugar, wine, and salt, beating until smooth. Yield: glaze for one 13- x 9-inch cake.

ICE CREAM CAKE

3 (3-ounce) packages
    ladyfingers, split lengthwise
½ gallon vanilla ice cream,
    softened and divided
1 (6-ounce) can frozen orange
    juice concentrate, undiluted
2 (10-ounce) packages frozen
    raspberries, thawed
2 (8¼-ounce) cans crushed
    pineapple, drained
2 teaspoons lemon juice
3 tablespoons chopped
    pistachio nuts
2 tablespoons finely chopped
    maraschino cherries
1 teaspoon almond
    extract
1 teaspoon rum flavoring
Whipped cream
Fresh whole strawberries

Line bottom and sides of a 9-inch springform pan with ladyfingers; set aside.

Combine 1 quart softened ice cream and orange juice concentrate in a medium mixing bowl, stirring well. Spoon mixture evenly into pan. Freeze.

Place raspberries in a medium saucepan; cook until thoroughly heated, stirring to crush berries. Strain, discarding seeds. Place raspberries, pineapple, and lemon juice in container of an electric blender. Process until smooth. Pour mixture into a medium mixing bowl; freeze until partially set. Beat at medium speed of an electric mixer 1 minute; spoon evenly over frozen ice cream mixture. Freeze.

Combine remaining ice cream, pistachio nuts, cherries, and flavorings in a large mixing bowl, stirring well. Spoon evenly over frozen raspberry mixture. Freeze overnight.

Remove from freezer 30 minutes before serving, and place in refrigerator. Remove sides of springform pan; place cake on a serving platter. Garnish with whipped cream and fresh strawberries. Yield: 12 servings.

*Bobby Jones, putting on
the ninth green at
1935 Masters Tournament.*

GOLF TEA AT JEKYLL ISLAND

Haute cuisine was one of the givens on Jekyll Island, playground of Northern society at the turn of the century. Some who wintered there brought their own cows (to assure the richest of milk). Others brought their private stock of terrapins and one came with fifty brace of pheasant imported from England. King Humbert of Italy, friend of J. Pierpont Morgan, sent several hundred wild boars as a gift; subsequently, boar hunting became prime sport. The old Rockefeller Cottage there became the Jekyll Island Museum. Teatime brought members off the greens to enjoy the music and to socialize over canapés and lemonade followed by fancy cakes or confections.

ENGLISH MUFFINS TOASTED WITH CHEESE BUTTER
HOT CHICKEN CANAPÉS
LEMON POUND CAKE
FRESH LEMONADE
ICED TEA

Serves 12

ENGLISH MUFFINS TOASTED WITH CHEESE BUTTER

½ cup butter, softened
1 cup (4 ounces) shredded sharp Cheddar cheese
1 teaspoon fresh lemon juice
¾ teaspoon Italian seasoning
⅛ teaspoon garlic powder
⅛ teaspoon pepper
6 English muffins, halved

Cream butter in a small mixing bowl; add remaining ingredients, except muffins, beating well. Spread butter mixture evenly over cut sides of muffins. Broil 3 to 4 inches from heating element until bubbly and lightly browned. Cut each muffin half into fourths. Yield: 12 appetizer servings.

HOT CHICKEN CANAPÉS

1 whole chicken breast, skinned, boned, and cooked
1 (8-ounce) package slivered almonds
⅓ cup chopped green onion
½ cup plus 2 tablespoons mayonnaise
⅛ teaspoon salt
Melba toast
Paprika

Grind together chicken and almonds in a small mixing bowl, using coarse blade of a meat grinder. Stir in onion, mayonnaise, and salt.

Spread 1 teaspoon chicken mixture on each piece of melba toast. Broil just until thoroughly heated. Sprinkle with paprika, and serve hot. Yield: about 12 appetizer servings.

Jekyll Island Club golf course from c.1910 postcard.

LEMON POUND CAKE

1 cup butter or margarine, softened
2⅔ cups sugar, divided
4 eggs
2 cups all-purpose flour
½ teaspoon baking powder
¼ teaspoon salt
½ cup evaporated milk
1 teaspoon vanilla extract
⅓ cup lemon juice
Notched lemon slices, cut in half

Cream butter in a large mixing bowl; gradually add 2 cups sugar, beating well. Add eggs, beating well.

Sift together flour, baking powder, and salt; add to creamed mixture alternately with milk, beginning and ending with flour mixture, mixing well. Stir in vanilla.

Pour batter into a well-greased 10-inch Bundt pan. Bake at 325° for 55 minutes or until cake tests done. Cool in pan on a wire rack 10 minutes; invert cake onto wire rack, and cool completely. Prick cake several times with a wooden pick. Combine remaining sugar and lemon juice in a small mixing bowl; pour over top of cake. Garnish with lemon slices. Yield: one 10-inch cake.

FRESH LEMONADE

1 quart freshly squeezed lemon juice (about 2 dozen lemons)
3 quarts water
3 cups sugar
Lemon twists

Combine all ingredients, except lemon twists, in a large container, stirring well. Chill.

Pour lemonade over ice in glasses, and garnish with lemon twists. Yield: about 1 gallon.

Variation: Three cups rum or vodka may be added to Fresh Lemonade, if desired.

Couples enjoying a tailgate picnic before the game, c.1905.

FOOTBALL TAILGATE PICNIC

The autumnal madness we call football brings out throngs of fans, and many of them know how to make their day complete: they ice down their favorite beverages and cook up a carload of their best traveling food. It takes energy in large doses to fuel a quarterback in the bleachers. Service at a tailgate lunch is somewhat informal; some keep a well-worn tablecloth (set aside for just such occasions) ready in the basket. Paper and plastic are nowhere more acceptable than at an easy tailgate lunch like this one with Chicken Nuggets and Lemon Sheet Cake. With good planning, very little has to be brought back home—just the memory of an occasion shared with family and friends.

SPICY CHICKEN NUGGETS
BACON-HORSERADISH DIP
VEGETABLES VINAIGRETTE
HEARTY ROLLS WITH
ASSORTED MEATS AND CHEESES
LEMON SHEET CAKE
FUDGE PIE
CHILLED COLAS

Serves 8

SPICY CHICKEN NUGGETS

10 chicken breast halves,
   skinned, boned, and cut
   into 1½-inch pieces
1½ cups buttermilk
2 eggs, beaten
1½ cups all-purpose flour
1¼ teaspoons salt
½ teaspoon red pepper
1 tablespoon garlic powder
2 teaspoons chili powder
¼ teaspoon dried whole
   thyme
¼ teaspoon paprika
Vegetable oil

Place chicken pieces in a shallow pan; combine buttermilk and eggs, and pour over chicken. Cover and refrigerate several hours.

Combine flour, salt, pepper, garlic powder, chili powder, thyme, and paprika in a medium mixing bowl; stir well. Drain chicken, and dredge each piece in flour mixture.

Heat 1 inch of oil in a large skillet to 375°. Add chicken in several batches, and fry 3 minutes or until golden brown, turning frequently. Add additional oil, if necessary. Drain well on paper towels. Yield: 8 servings.

Morton's Salt advertising blotter, c.1900.

VEGETABLES VINAIGRETTE

2 small tomatoes, peeled and
   cut into narrow wedges
2 cups broccoli flowerets
1 large onion, sliced and
   separated into rings
1 small zucchini, sliced
1 medium-size yellow squash,
   sliced
1 medium cucumber, sliced
1 cup olive oil
⅓ cup white wine vinegar
2 cloves garlic, minced
2 teaspoons dried whole
   oregano
½ teaspoon dry mustard
1 teaspoon salt
½ teaspoon pepper

Combine first 6 ingredients; toss lightly.

Combine oil, vinegar, garlic, oregano, mustard, salt, and pepper in a jar; cover tightly and shake well. Pour over vegetables, and toss lightly. Cover and refrigerate overnight. Serve vegetables with a slotted spoon. Yield: 8 servings.

Wheatena cereal ad, c.1925. "They don't grow this way on lollipops!"

BACON-HORSERADISH DIP

1 (16-ounce) carton
   commercial sour cream
2 tablespoons half-and-half
2 tablespoons prepared
   horseradish
2 tablespoons finely chopped
   green onion tops
4 slices bacon, cooked and
   crumbled
½ teaspoon salt
Corn chips

Combine sour cream and half-and-half, mixing well; add horseradish, onion, bacon, and salt, reserving 1 tablespoon bacon. Stir well. Cover and refrigerate overnight.

Sprinkle reserved bacon over dip. Serve with corn chips. Yield: about 2 cups.

The first University of Alabama football team, 1892.

HEARTY ROLLS

2 packages dry yeast
1 tablespoon plus 2
  teaspoons sugar, divided
¾ cup warm water (105° to
  115°)
¾ cup milk
⅓ cup butter or margarine,
  melted
1½ teaspoons salt
2 teaspoons cracked black
  pepper
1 egg, beaten
1½ cups (6 ounces) shredded
  sharp Cheddar cheese
4½ to 5 cups all-purpose
  flour, divided
Additional melted butter
Sesame seeds
Assorted meats and cheeses

Dissolve yeast and 1 teaspoon sugar in water in a large mixing bowl; stir well, and let stand 5 minutes or until bubbly.

Add remaining sugar, milk, ⅓ cup butter, salt, pepper, egg, and cheese to yeast mixture; stir

well. Add 2 cups flour, stirring well. Stir in enough remaining flour to make a firm dough.

Turn dough out onto a lightly floured surface; knead 8 to 10 minutes or until smooth and elastic. Cover and let rise in a warm place (85°), free from drafts, 45 minutes or until doubled in bulk.

Punch dough down; let rest 15 minutes. Turn dough out onto a lightly floured surface. Divide into 20 equal portions, shaping each into a ball. Arrange rolls in a greased 13- x 9- x 2-inch baking pan. Brush lightly with additional butter; sprinkle with sesame seeds. Cover with a floured towel. Repeat rising procedure 45 minutes or until doubled in bulk.

Bake at 375° for 20 minutes or until golden brown. Serve hot with assorted meats and cheese. Yield: 20 rolls.

Football started at Eton, Rugby, and other English schools, each with its own set of rules. Two main games evolved: association football (soccer) and rugby, in which a runner could carry the ball and be tackled. In 1871, English clubs formed the Rugby Football Union and adopted standards. American football was more like association football until the Harvard team visited Canada in the 1870s and liked the rugby rules. In 1873, Harvard and other Ivy League colleges met to lay the foundation for intercollegiate games as we know them.

LEMON SHEET CAKE

½ cup butter or margarine, softened
2 cups sugar
6 egg yolks
2½ cups all-purpose flour
2 teaspoons baking powder
½ teaspoon salt
1 cup milk
Grated rind and juice of 1 lemon
Lemon Cream Frosting
Lemon bows

Cream butter in a large mixing bowl; gradually add sugar, beating well. Add egg yolks, one at a time, beating well.

Combine flour, baking powder, and salt; add to creamed mixture alternately with milk, beginning and ending with flour mixture. Stir well after each addition. Stir in lemon rind and juice.

Pour batter into a well-greased and floured 13- x 9- x 2-inch baking pan. Bake at 350° for 35 minutes or until a wooden pick inserted in center comes out clean. Cool completely in pan on a wire rack.

Spread Lemon Cream Frosting over cake. Garnish with lemon bows. Yield: one 13- x 9-inch cake.

Lemon Cream Frosting:

¼ cup butter or margarine, softened
1 (16-ounce) package powdered sugar, sifted and divided
¼ cup whipping cream
Grated rind and juice of 1 lemon
5 drops yellow food coloring

Combine butter and 2 cups sugar, beating well. Add remaining sugar, whipping cream, lemon rind and juice, and food coloring; beat until smooth. Yield: frosting for one 13- x 9-inch cake.

If Fudge Pie did not come in wedges, someone might declare he was eating brownies.

FUDGE PIE

1 cup sugar
⅓ cup all-purpose flour
½ cup butter or margarine, melted
½ cup cocoa
¾ cup water
2 eggs
Toasted pecan halves

Combine sugar and flour in a large mixing bowl, stirring well.

Stir in melted butter.

Combine cocoa, water, and eggs; beat well. Pour into sugar mixture, stirring well.

Pour mixture into a buttered 9-inch pieplate. Bake at 350° for 35 minutes or until set. Garnish pie with pecan halves. Cool completely, and slice. Yield: one 9-inch pie.

TEXAS-OKLAHOMA WEEKEND PARTY

Dallasites may split their allegiance for the Cotton Bowl, but when Oklahoma comes to town the first Saturday in October (which is also the first Saturday of the State Fair of Texas), the "Big D" presents a solid front. University of Texas football fans, from alumni and students to the man in the street, know war is inevitable. Naturally, parties abound. One U.T. alumnus starts a cocktail party the day before the game, and it has been known to last until just before game time. Everything in sight, from decorations to food, is orange and white, University of Texas colors. With a menu like this, of course, nobody wants to leave the party!

BOILED SHRIMP WITH COCKTAIL SAUCE
SMOKY SALMON SPREAD
CHEDDAR CHEESE MOUNDS
TEXAS CAVIAR
ROAST BEEF TENDERLOIN
SWEET POTATO BUNS
BOURBON PEACHES
ORANGE TARTS

Serves 16

BOILED SHRIMP WITH COCKTAIL SAUCE

1 tablespoon plus 1 teaspoon
  caraway seeds
2 quarts water
1 tablespoon plus 1 teaspoon
  salt
4 pounds uncooked medium
  shrimp
Commercial cocktail sauce

Tie caraway seeds in a cheese-cloth bag.

Combine water and salt in a large Dutch oven. Add cheese-cloth bag. Cover and bring to a boil; boil 5 minutes. Uncover and add shrimp; simmer 3 minutes. Drain, discarding cheese-cloth bag.

Peel and devein shrimp. Serve shrimp hot or chilled with cocktail sauce. Yield: 16 appetizer servings.

SMOKY SALMON SPREAD

1 (16-ounce) can red salmon,
  drained and flaked
1 (8-ounce) package cream
  cheese, softened
1 medium onion, grated
½ cup finely chopped
  walnuts
1 teaspoon pickle relish,
  drained
1 teaspoon liquid smoke
½ teaspoon lemon juice
Assorted crackers

Combine all ingredients, except crackers, in a medium mixing bowl; mix well. Chill overnight. Serve with assorted crackers. Yield: 4 cups.

*Football fans on the
fourth yard line stand
and cheer on their
team, c.1904.*

CHEDDAR CHEESE MOUNDS

1 cup butter, softened
2½ cups (10 ounces)
  shredded sharp Cheddar
  cheese
2 cups all-purpose flour
2 cups puffed rice
  cereal
¼ teaspoon Worcestershire
  sauce
¼ teaspoon hot sauce

Cream butter and cheese in a medium mixing bowl. Add remaining ingredients; mix well.

Drop cheese mixture by heaping teaspoonfuls 1 inch apart onto greased baking sheets. Bake at 325° for 20 minutes or until lightly browned. Remove from baking sheets, and cool on wire racks. Yield: about 5½ dozen.

TEXAS CAVIAR

2 large tomatoes, finely
  chopped
3 green onions, chopped
2 jalapeño peppers, chopped
1 tablespoon jalapeño pepper
  juice
1 (4½-ounce) can chopped
  black olives, drained
1 (4-ounce) can chopped
  green chiles, drained
3 tablespoons olive oil
1½ teaspoons
  vinegar
1 teaspoon garlic salt
Salt and pepper to taste
Tortilla chips

Combine first 9 ingredients in a large mixing bowl; mix well. Stir in salt and pepper to taste; refrigerate 5 hours or overnight. Serve with tortilla chips. Yield: about 3 cups.

ROAST BEEF TENDERLOIN

1 (5- to 7-pound) beef
  tenderloin, trimmed
2 tablespoons olive oil
1 tablespoon salt
½ teaspoon freshly ground
  black pepper
¼ teaspoon red pepper
1 small carrot, scraped and
  sliced
1 tablespoon finely chopped
  onion
¼ cup lemon juice
1 (10¾-ounce) can beef broth,
  diluted

Rub tenderloin with oil, salt, and pepper. Place carrot and onion in bottom of a shallow roasting pan. Place tenderloin on vegetables. Tuck narrow end under to make roast more uniformly thick. Pour lemon juice over tenderloin; cover and marinate at least 3 hours.

Pour broth into pan; insert meat thermometer in tenderloin, if desired. Bake, uncovered, at 500° for 5 minutes; reduce heat, and continue baking, uncovered, at 350° for 55 minutes or until thermometer registers 140° (rare). Cut into thin slices. Yield: 16 servings.

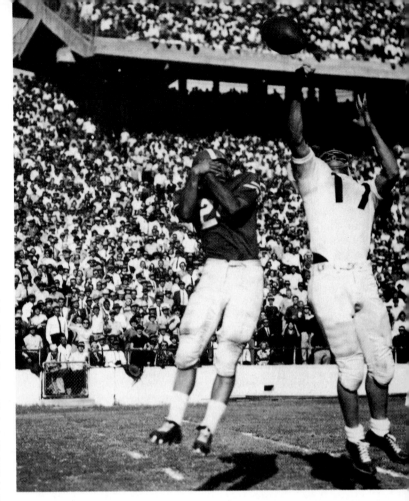

Of all the sports Southerners flock to see, none involves the investment of more emotion than intercollegiate football. An elephant is an absent-minded mouse compared with a college alumnus, with his total recall of old rivalries. He can recount, play-by-play, every game his team has played since he was a lowly undergrad. Loyal to the core, he will drive anywhere and sit through any weather to be with his team. Football season is a time to get together with old friends and have a party.

SWEET POTATO BUNS

3 cups all-purpose flour
3 cups whole wheat
  flour
2 packages dry yeast
1½ cups warm water (105°
  to 115°)
⅓ cup firmly packed brown
  sugar
½ cup butter or margarine,
  softened
2 eggs
1 (16-ounce) can cut sweet
  potatoes, drained
1¼ teaspoons salt

Combine flour in a large mixing bowl, stirring well; set aside.

Combine yeast and warm water in container of an electric blender; process until yeast is dissolved.

While blender is processing, add sugar, butter, eggs, sweet potatoes, salt, and 1 cup flour mixture. Process until smooth.

Add sweet potato mixture to remaining flour mixture, stirring to form a soft dough.

Turn dough out onto a lightly floured surface, and knead 5 minutes or until smooth and elastic. Place in a greased bowl, turning to grease top. Cover tightly and refrigerate 6 hours or overnight.

Shape dough into 32 balls. Place balls 3 inches apart on greased baking sheets. Cover and let rise in a warm place (85°), free from drafts, 1 hour or until doubled in bulk.

Bake at 350° for 20 minutes or until buns are lightly browned and sound hollow when tapped. Remove buns from baking sheets; cool on wire racks. Split and use as sandwich buns. Yield: 32 buns.

A critical moment in
Texas versus Oklahoma
game that was played
in Dallas in 1955.

BOURBON PEACHES

3½ quarts water,
 divided
1 tablespoon ascorbic-citric
 powder
6 pounds peaches
6 cups sugar
4 strips orange rind
3 cups bourbon

Combine 2 quarts water and ascorbic-citric powder in a large mixing bowl; set aside.

Peel peaches; slice each in half, and remove pit. Place peach halves in reserved water mixture.

Combine remaining water and sugar in a large saucepan; bring to a boil. Drain peaches. Add one-fourth of peach halves to boiling syrup; reduce heat, and simmer 5 minutes.

Remove peach halves with a slotted spoon; pack into hot sterilized jars, leaving ½-inch headspace. Repeat procedure with remaining peaches, reserving syrup. Place a strip of orange rind in each jar.

Cook reserved syrup until mixture reaches 220° on a candy thermometer; remove from heat, and let cool 5 minutes. Place 3 cups syrup in a small saucepan, discarding remaining syrup; add bourbon, stirring well. Place over medium heat, and cook until thoroughly heated.

Pour over peaches in jars, leaving ½-inch headspace; wipe rims clean. Cover at once with metal lids, and screw bands tight. Process in boiling-water bath 20 minutes. Yield: 4 pints.

Note: Chilled Bourbon Peaches may be spooned over softened cream cheese and served with unsalted crackers.

*Nineteenth-century
bourbon label features
a whiskey still in the
midst of a peach orchard.*

ORANGE TARTS

1 cup sugar
2 tablespoons cornstarch
½ teaspoon salt
1 cup orange juice
1 cup water
¼ cup lemon juice
3 eggs, separated
2 tablespoons grated orange
 rind
1 tablespoon butter or
 margarine
1 drop red food coloring
Tart shells
¼ cup plus 2 tablespoons
 sugar

Combine 1 cup sugar, cornstarch, and salt in top of a non-aluminum double boiler. Gradually add orange juice, water, lemon juice, and egg yolks; stir until smooth. Cook over boiling water, stirring constantly, until thickened and smooth. Remove from heat; stir in orange rind, butter, and food coloring, mixing well. Spoon filling into prepared tart shells.

Beat egg whites (at room temperature) until foamy. Gradually add ¼ cup plus 2 tablespoons sugar, 1 tablespoon at a time, beating until stiff peaks form. Spread 1 tablespoon meringue over each tart, sealing to edge of pastry. Bake at 350° for 10 to 12 minutes or until meringue is golden brown. Cool tarts to room temperature; chill. Yield: 16 tarts.

Tart Shells:

3 cups all-purpose
 flour
1 teaspoon salt
1 cup shortening
¼ cup plus 2 tablespoons
 cold water

Combine flour and salt in a medium mixing bowl; cut in shortening with a pastry blender until mixture resembles coarse meal. Sprinkle water evenly over surface; stir with a fork until dry ingredients are moistened. Shape dough into a ball; chill.

Divide dough into 16 equal portions. Roll each portion to ⅛-inch thickness on a lightly floured surface. Press each portion into a 4-inch tart pan. Prick bottom and sides of pastry shells with a fork. Bake at 425° for 10 to 12 minutes or until lightly browned. Yield: 16 tart shells.

Aerial view of the Sugar Bowl in New Orleans.

SUGAR BOWL FARE AT BUSTER HOLMES

On January 1, 1935, Tulane trounced Temple in the Inaugural Sugar Bowl football classic in New Orleans. It was a triumph for the city, culminating six years of work. Forty years later, Alabama's Crimson Tide celebrated the opening of the Superdome by beating Penn State, winning its first bowl game since 1967. For many of those years, one of the best-known watering holes in the French Quarter has been Buster Holmes Restaurant on Burgundy Street. Football players and fans flock to Buster's place for fine Southern cooking. His menu, made up daily and written on notebook paper, always includes his famous Red Beans and Rice presented here.

 BUSTER'S RED BEANS AND RICE
FRENCH BREAD
FRESH APPLE CAKE

Serves 6 to 8

BUSTER'S RED BEANS AND RICE

1 pound dried red beans
2 quarts water
1 (1-pound) ham hock
1 large onion, chopped
1 large green pepper, seeded and chopped
2 large cloves garlic, minced
¼ cup butter or margarine
Salt and pepper to taste
Hot sauce
Hot cooked rice

Sort and wash beans. Combine beans and water in a large stockpot; bring to a boil. Reduce heat to medium; cover and cook 40 minutes.

Add ham hock, onion, green pepper, garlic, and butter. Reduce heat; cover and simmer 2 hours, stirring occasionally.

Mash most of beans against sides of stockpot with back of a spoon; stir well. Cover and bring to a boil; reduce heat to medium-high. Cook, uncovered, 1 hour or until desired consistency, stirring occasionally. Add salt and pepper to taste. Serve beans with hot sauce over rice. Yield: 6 to 8 servings.

FRESH APPLE CAKE

3 cups all-purpose flour
1½ teaspoons baking soda
½ teaspoon salt
1 teaspoon ground cinnamon
2 eggs
2 cups sugar
1¼ cups vegetable oil
2 teaspoons vanilla extract
5 medium-size cooking apples, peeled, cored, and finely chopped
1 cup chopped pecans
Whipped cream (optional)

Sift together flour, soda, salt, and cinnamon; set aside.

Beat eggs in a large mixing bowl until foamy; gradually add sugar, beating until thickened. Add oil and vanilla, beating well. Add flour mixture; beat well. Stir in apples and pecans.

Spoon batter into a greased and floured 10-inch tube pan. Bake at 350° for 1 hour and 20 minutes or until a wooden pick inserted near center comes out clean. Cool in pan on a wire rack 15 minutes; remove cake from pan, and let cool completely. Serve with whipped cream, if desired. Yield: one 10-inch cake.

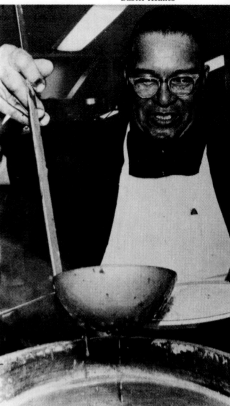

Buster Holmes (above) ladling up his famous Red Beans and Rice (below), served with French bread.

SCOTTISH HIGHLAND GAMES PICNIC

I f you trace your lineage back to Scotland on the paternal side and maybe your surname begins with Mac (meaning son of), you already know where to go in mid-July: Grandfather Mountain, at Linville, North Carolina. Over one hundred clans come together then for the games, sports, dancing, and ceremonies that are part of the Scottish heritage. Children learn that bagpipes make fascinating music and that "forfar bridies" are what you call meat pies when you're wearing the tartan. Best of all is the caber tossing. In old days, a young tree was the caber; now it looks like a telephone pole. Men balance it on end and toss it as far as they possibly can.

SCOTTISH MEAT PIES
SAUSAGE CORNBREAD STICKS
SCOTCH EGGS
SCOTTISH POTATO SALAD
SHORTBREAD SQUARES
OATMEAL COOKIES
ICED TEA
ALE or DARK BEER

Serves 6

SCOTTISH MEAT PIES

½ pound round steak, cut into ½-inch cubes
1 large potato, peeled and cubed
1 medium onion, chopped
½ cup diced carrots
1 teaspoon salt
⅛ teaspoon pepper
Pastry (recipe follows)
2 tablespoons butter or margarine, divided
2 tablespoons water, divided
Milk
Prepared hot mustard

Combine first six ingredients in a large mixing bowl; mix well. Set aside.

Divide pastry into 6 equal portions; roll each portion into a circle, 8 inches in diameter. Place ¾ cup beef mixture on each pastry circle. Dot with 1 teaspoon butter, and sprinkle with 1 teaspoon water. Fold pastry circle in half, making edges even. Using a fork, press edges of pastry together to seal. Brush each pie with milk.

Place on baking sheets, and bake at 375° for 55 minutes or until browned. Serve warm with mustard. Yield: 6 servings.

Pastry:

3 cups all-purpose flour
1½ teaspoons salt
½ cup lard
5 to 6 tablespoons cold water

Combine flour and salt in a small mixing bowl; cut in lard with a pastry blender until mixture resembles coarse meal. Sprinkle water evenly over surface of flour mixture; stir with a fork until dry ingredients are moistened. Shape dough into a ball; chill. Use as directed. Yield: pastry for 6 miniature pies.

San Antonio lassie, c.1925.

Institute of Texan Cultures

SAUSAGE CORNBREAD STICKS

2 cups self-rising cornmeal
1 teaspoon sugar
1½ cups milk
1 egg, beaten
¼ cup shortening, melted
1 pound bulk pork sausage

Combine cornmeal and sugar in a medium mixing bowl; mix well. Stir in milk, egg, and shortening just until dry ingredients are moistened. Set aside.

Brown sausage in a large skillet over medium heat, stirring to crumble. Drain well. Stir sausage into cornmeal mixture.

Heat well-greased cast-iron corn stick pans in a 450° oven 3 minutes or until very hot. Pour batter into pans, filling two-thirds full. Bake at 450° for 20 minutes or until golden brown. Yield: about 1½ dozen.

Scotch Eggs (front), Sausage Cornbread Sticks (center), and Scottish Meat Pies. Scottish Potato Salad (right) has beets for color and herbs for mystery.

Photographer: Hugh Morton, Grandfather Mountain

The Gathering of the Clans would not be authentic without winded bagpipes and kilted Scotsmen.

SCOTCH EGGS

1 cup ground, cooked ham
⅓ cup fine dry breadcrumbs
⅓ cup milk
½ teaspoon prepared mustard
⅛ teaspoon red pepper
1 egg, beaten
6 hard-cooked eggs
Vegetable oil

Combine ham, breadcrumbs, milk, mustard, pepper, and beaten egg in a small mixing bowl; stir until well blended. Cover with plastic wrap, and chill 15 minutes. Pat ham mixture evenly around each hard-cooked egg. Cover with plastic wrap, and chill 1 hour.

Using a frying basket, fry 2 eggs at a time in deep, hot oil (350°) for 2 minutes or until lightly browned. Drain well on paper towels. Serve immediately. Yield: 6 servings.

SCOTTISH POTATO SALAD

12 medium potatoes (about 4 pounds), cleaned
1 cup diced, cooked beets
1 cup shelled fresh green peas, cooked
⅓ cup white wine vinegar
⅓ cup olive oil
1 green onion, chopped
1 teaspoon chopped fresh tarragon
1 teaspoon chopped fresh chervil
1 teaspoon chopped fresh parsley
1 teaspoon salt
½ teaspoon pepper

Cook potatoes in boiling water to cover 25 minutes or until tender. Drain well, and cool slightly. Peel potatoes, and cut into 1-inch cubes. Set aside.

Combine potatoes, beets, and peas in a large mixing bowl; toss gently until well blended. Combine vinegar, olive oil, onion, tarragon, chervil, parsley, salt, and pepper in a jar; cover and shake vigorously until well blended. Pour over potato mixture, and toss gently until well blended. Chill until ready to serve. Yield: 6 servings.

SHORTBREAD SQUARES

2 cups butter, softened
2 cups sugar
4 cups sifted bread flour or all-purpose flour

Cream butter in a large mixing bowl; gradually add sugar, beating until light and fluffy. Gradually add flour, beating until thoroughly blended.

Press mixture into a 15- x 10- x 1-inch jellyroll pan; prick surface with tines of a fork. Bake at 300° for 50 minutes or until lightly browned. Cool completely in pan. Cut into 2-inch squares. Yield: about 3 dozen.

OATMEAL COOKIES

¾ cup shortening
1 cup firmly packed brown sugar
½ cup sugar
1 egg
¼ cup water
1 teaspoon vanilla extract
1 cup all-purpose flour
½ teaspoon baking soda
1 teaspoon salt
2 cups quick-cooking oats, uncooked

Cream shortening in a large mixing bowl; gradually add sugar, beating well. Add egg, water, and vanilla, beating well.

Sift together flour, soda, and salt in a small mixing bowl; add to creamed mixture, stirring until well blended. Add oats, mixing well.

Drop batter by heaping teaspoonfuls 3 inches apart onto lightly greased cookie sheets. Bake at 350° for 12 to 15 minutes or until lightly browned. Remove from cookie sheets, and let cool completely on wire racks. Yield: about 5 dozen.

The Caber Toss at the Highland Games, held at Grandfather Mountain, Linville, North Carolina.

ACKNOWLEDGMENTS

Amaretto Mousse courtesy of Evelyn McKinney, Camden, South Carolina.

Barbecued Beef courtesy of the Extension Foods and Nutrition Specialists, Texas A&M University, College Station, Texas.

Barbecued Beef Brisket, Carrot Cupcakes, Green Tomato Pie adapted from *Revel* by The Junior League of Shreveport, ©1980. By permission of The Junior League of Shreveport, Inc., Louisiana.

Barbecued Venison Steaks adapted from *Gourmet of the Delta*, collected by St. John's Woman's Auxiliary and St. Paul's Woman's Auxiliary, ©1964. By permission of St. John's Woman's Auxiliary, Leland, Mississippi.

Buffalo Roast, Easy Barbecue Sauce courtesy of The Frank Phillips Foundation, Inc., Woolaroc Lodge, Bartlesville, Oklahoma.

Caviar Ring, Dressed Asparagus, Horseshoe Cheese Mold, Marinated Beef Tenderloin courtesy of Jack Brantley, Camden, South Carolina.

Cheddar Cheese Mounds by Debbie Deering Owen, Smoky Salmon Spread by Louise Stromberg Bates, Texas Caviar by Jan Bixler Bennett and Theresa Valenta Pesek adapted from *Cook 'em Horns!* by The Ex-Students' Association of the University of Texas, ©1981. By permission of The Ex-Students' Association of the University of Texas, Austin.

Cheese Straws, Monogrammed Petits Fours courtesy of Lane Garity, Camden, South Carolina.

Chocolate Chip Pie adapted from *Fascinating Foods from the Deep South* by Alline P. Van Duzor, ©1963. By permission of Crown Publishing Company, New York.

Cold Roast Quail with Savory Orange Sauce, Herbed Tomato Consommé, Hot Spiced Compote, Waldorf Salad with Wine courtesy of Joyce Pervier, Joyce Sherrer, and Iva Welton of Rose Hill Plantation, Hilton Head Island, South Carolina.

Duck Gumbo adapted from a prize-winning recipe from the Stuttgart, Arkansas, Duck-Calling Contest.

Fresh Peach Cake, Marinated Tomato Salad adapted from *Caterin' to Charleston* by Gloria Mann Maynard, Meredith Maynard Chase, and Holly Maynard Jenkins, ©1981. By permission of Merritt Publishing Co., Charleston, South Carolina.

Fresh Vegetable Salad courtesy of Martha S. Hayes, Jemison, Alabama.

Game meats provided by Rick Fernambucq, Pelham, Alabama.

Meal-in-a-Sandwich adapted from *Huntsville Heritage Cookbook* by The Grace Club Auxiliary, ©1967. By permission of The Grace Club Auxiliary, Inc., Huntsville, Alabama.

Menu for "Belle Meade Hunt Breakfast" courtesy of Susanne D. Painter, Augusta, Georgia.

Menu for "Brunch Before the Masters" adapted from recipes from *Tea-Time at the Masters* by the Junior League of Augusta, ©1977. By permission of the Junior League of Augusta, Georgia.

Menu for "Game Fish Celebration in Pensacola" adapted from recipes from the Sixth Annual Pensacola International Billfish Tournament.

Menu for "Hunters' Breakfast in Thomasville" adapted from recipes from *Pines and Plantations* by the Vashti Auxiliary, ©1976. By permission of the Vashti Auxiliary, Thomasville, Georgia.

Menu for "Point-to-Point Picnic at Winterthur" courtesy of Anne B. Coleman, Winterthur Museum and Gardens, Winterthur, Delaware.

Menu for "Spectator Sport at Oaklawn," Old-Fashioned Kentucky Burgoo courtesy of Turf Catering, Larry Wolken, Director, Hot Springs, Arkansas.

Menu for "Sugar Bowl Fare at Buster Holmes" courtesy of Buster Holmes Restaurant, New Orleans, Louisiana.

Menu for "Tennis Championship Party" adapted from recipes from *Le Bontemps* by the Young Women's Christian Organization, ©1982. By permission of the Young Women's Christian Organization, Baton Rouge, Louisiana.

Mint Juleps courtesy of The Kentucky Distillers Association, Frankfort, Kentucky.

Parmesan Scalloped Tomatoes adapted from *Georgia Heritage: Treasured Recipes* by The National Society of The Colonial Dames of America in the State of Georgia, ©1979. By permission of the Andrew Low House, Savannah, Georgia.

Pecan Cheese Ball adapted from a recipe by the Georgia Pecan Growers Association.

Pensacola Layered Salad adapted from *A Dash of Sevillity* by The Pensacola Heritage Foundation, ©1971. By permission of The Pensacola Heritage Foundation, Florida.

Pheasant aux Fines Herbes adapted from *The Wild Game Cookbook* by The National American Hunting Club, ©1983. By permission of NAHC, Minneapolis, Minnesota.

Ragout of Venison, Smoked Duck adapted from *South Carolina Wildlife Cookbook* by Julie Lumpkin and Nancy Ann Coleman, 1982. Published by *South Carolina Wildlife* magazine. By permission of South Carolina Wildlife & Marines Resources Department, Columbia, South Carolina.

Savannah Salad courtesy of Mrs. Bailee Kronowitz, Savannah, Georgia.

Savory Stuffed Squash courtesy of Mrs. James Edwards, Grove Hill, Alabama.

Sweet Potato Buns adapted from *Flavor Favorites!*, edited by Marilyn Wyrick Ingram, ©1979. By permission of Baylor University Alumni, Baylor University, Waco, Texas.

Wild Rice and Cheese Casserole adapted from *Southern Sideboards*, compiled by The Junior League of Jackson, ©1978. By permission of The Junior League of Jackson, Mississippi.

Art for back cover from the collection of Kit Barry, Brattleboro, Vermont.

INDEX

Almond Coleslaw, 74
Almond Lace Wafers, 84
Amaretto Mousse, 13
Appetizers
  Canapés, Hot Chicken, 123
  Caviar Ring, 11
  Caviar, Texas, 129
  Celery, Stuffed, 75
  Cheese Ball, Pecan, 92
  Cheese Dreams, 23
  Cheese Heart, Herbed, 80
  Cheese Mold, Horseshoe, 10
  Cheese Mounds, Cheddar, 129
  Cheese Puffs, 118
  Cheese Straws, 12
  Dip, Bacon-Horseradish, 125
  Dip with Vegetables, Herb, 22
  English Muffins Toasted with
    Cheese Butter, 123
  Mushrooms, Herbed, 11
  Shrimp, Chilled Pickled, 22
  Shrimp with Cocktail Sauce,
    Boiled, 129
  Spinach Balls, 23
  Spread, Smoky Salmon, 129
Apples
  Cake, Fresh Apple, 133
  Casserole, Apple, 48
  Slices, Fried Apple, 56
Applesauce à la Mode, 34
Asparagus, Dressed, 12

Bacon-Horseradish Dip, 125
Barbecue
  Beef, Barbecued, 34
  Beef Brisket, Barbecued, 72
  Marlin, Barbecued, 106
  Pinto Beans, Barbecued, 72
  Sauce, Barbecue, 72
  Sauce, Easy Barbecue, 52
  Spareribs, Barbecued, 68
  Venison Steaks, Barbecued, 52
Beans
  Beer Beans, 34
  Green Beans Amandine, 55
  Kidney Bean Salad, 69
  Pinto Beans, Barbecued, 72
  Pork and Beans, Campfire, 95

Red Beans and Rice,
  Buster's, 133
  Salad, Cold Bean, 89
  Vegetable Casserole, 93
Béarnaise Sauce, 24
Beef
  Barbecued Beef, 34
  Brisket, Barbecued Beef, 72
  Calf Fries, 35
  Campers' Stew, 76
  Frankfurters with
    Condiments, 95
  Marinated Beef Tenderloin, 11
  Meal-in-a-Sandwich, 74
  Meat Pies, Scottish, 134
  Rib Eyes, Broiled, 35
  Roast Beef Tenderloin, 130
  Salad, Cold Roast Beef, 92
  Sandwiches, Corned Beef, 17
  Stew, Big-Batch Beef, 78
Beer Beans, 34
Beverages
  Alcoholic
    Bloody Bulls, 117
    Bloody Marys, 24
    Mint Juleps, 21
    Punch, Champagne 112
    Punch, Winterthur, 18
    Wine Spritzers, 116
  Lemonade, Fresh, 123
  Orange Juice, Spiced, 77
  Punch with Ice Ring, Fruit, 26
  Tea, Fruited Iced, 20
Biscuits, Bran, 51
Biscuits, Sweet, 28
Blackberry Cobbler, Quick, 103
Bloody Bulls, 117
Bloody Marys, 24
Bourbon
  Ham, Bourbon-Glazed, 118
  Peaches, Bourbon, 131
  Peaches over Frozen Custard,
    Bourbon-Blazed, 93
  Sauce, Bread and Butter
    Pudding with Bourbon, 15
Breads. See also specific types.
  Cheese Puffs, 118
  Croutons, Butter-Toasted, 83

Garlic Bread, 51
Garlic Bread, Grilled, 77, 90
Toast, Texas, 34
Yeast
  French Bread, 32, 59
  French Bread, Herbed, 84
  French Bread, Sour, 120
  Herb Bread, 20
  Rye Bread, Dark, 17
  Zucchini Bread, 120
Broccoli, Soup, 18
Buffalo Roast, 52
Burgoo, Old-Fashioned
  Kentucky, 15
Butterscotch Brownies, 75

Cakes
  Apple Cake, Fresh, 133
  Carrot Cupcakes, 73
  Cream Cake, Italian, 90
  Ice Cream Cake, 121
  Lemon Sheet Cake, 127
  Oatmeal Cake with Coconut
    Topping, 70
  Peach Cake, Fresh, 81
  Petits Fours, Monogrammed, 13
  Pound Cake, Lemon, 123
  Pound Cake, Orange-Glazed
    Pecan, 98
Calf Fries, 35
Carrots
  Cupcakes, Carrot, 73
  Soufflé, Carrot, 118
  Sweet-and-Sour Carrots, 64
Casseroles
  Apple Casserole, 48
  Egg Casserole, 118
  Vegetable Casserole, 93
  Wild Rice and Cheese
    Casserole, 42
Catfish, Fried, 61
Caviar Ring, 11
Caviar, Texas, 129
Celery, Stuffed, 75
Cheese
  Ball, Pecan Cheese, 92
  Butter, English Muffins Toasted
    with Cheese, 123

Cheese *(continued)*
  Casserole, Wild Rice and
    Cheese, 42
  Dreams, Cheese, 23
  Grits, Cheese, 26
  Herbed Cheese Heart, 80
  Mold, Horseshoe Cheese, 10
  Mounds, Cheddar Cheese, 129
  Potatoes, Cheese, 55
  Puffs, Cheese, 118
  Sandwiches, Pimiento
    Cheese, 100
  Straws, Cheese, 12
  Tomatoes, Parmesan
    Scalloped, 51
Cherry Squares, 59
Chicken
  Breasts, Lemon Chicken, 18
  Canapés, Hot Chicken, 123
  Fried Chicken, Buttermilk, 82
  Fried Chicken, Crisp Oven-, 99
  Grilled Chicken, 55
  Nuggets, Spicy Chicken, 125
Chocolate
  Brownies, Chewy, 107
  Fudge Pie, 127
  Pie, Chocolate Chip, 70
  Pie, Chocolate Refrigerator, 43
  S'Mores, 95
Chutney, Tomato, 47
Coconut
  Squares, Toasted Coconut, 77
  Topping, Coconut, 70
Coleslaw
  Almond Coleslaw, 74
  Coleslaw, 61, 89
  Summer Slaw, 106
Cookies
  Almond Lace Wafers, 84
  Lace Cookies, French, 116
  Oatmeal Cookies, 136
  Pecan Icebox Cookies, 23
  Shortbread Squares, 136
  Sugar Cookies, 45, 100
Corn, Grilled, 97
Corn Grilled in Husks, 89
Corn Relish Salad, 69
Cornbreads
  Corn Pone, 56
  Corn Sticks, 15
  Crackling Cornbread, 78
  Dressing, Mushroom
    Cornbread, 64
  Hush Puppies, 61
  Muffins, Cornmeal, 103
  Sausage Cornbread Sticks, 134
  Southern Cornbread, 42
Crab Cake Sandwiches,
  Chesapeake Bay, 28
Crabs, Steamed, 92
Cranberry-Orange Relish, 43
Croutons, Butter-Toasted, 83
Cucumber Soup, Cold, 114

Date-Nut Squares, 48
Desserts
  Apple Casserole, 48
  Applesauce à la Mode, 34
  Apple Slices, Fried, 56
  Brownies, Butterscotch, 75

Brownies, Chewy, 107
Cherry Squares, 59
Chess Bars, Lemon-Glazed, 90
Coconut Squares, Toasted, 77
Compote, Hot Spiced, 32
Custard, Frozen, 93
Custard Sauce over Strawberries
  and Raspberries, Chilled, 84
Date-Nut Squares, 48
Devil Dogs, 45
Lemon Parfait, 116
Molasses Spice Bars, 17
Mousse, Amaretto, 13
Oranges in Wine Sauce, 20
Peaches, Bourbon, 131
Peaches over Frozen Custard,
  Bourbon-Blazed, 93
Pudding with Bourbon Sauce,
  Bread and Butter, 15
S'Mores, 95
Strawberries with Rich
  Cream, 23
Strawberry Sauce over Vanilla Ice
  Cream, 56
Strawberry Shortcake, 28
Wine Bars, 121
Dewberry Cobbler, 37
Dill Marinade, 114
Dill Shrimp, 114
Dove, Plantation, 50
Dressing, Mushroom
  Cornbread, 64
Dressing, Wild Duck, 42
Duck
  Dressing, Wild Duck, 42
  Gumbo, Duck, 59
  Smoked Duck, 40

Eggs
  Belle Meade Specials, 24
  Casserole, Egg, 118
  Chausseur, Eggs, 47
  Deviled Eggs, 75
  Lobster-Stuffed Eggs, 111
  Scotch Eggs, 136
English Muffins Toasted with
  Cheese Butter, 123

Fish Stew, 102
Frankfurters with Condiments, 95
Frostings, Fillings, and Toppings
  Coconut Topping, 70
  Lemon Cream Frosting, 127
  Orange Glaze, 98
  Royal Icing, 13
Fruit. *See also* specific types.
  Compote, Hot Spiced, 32
  Ginger Fruit Cups, 26
  Punch with Ice Ring, Fruit, 26
  Salad, Fruit, 78
  Tarts, Glazed Fruit, 112
Fudge Pie, 127

Garlic Bread, 51
Garlic Bread, Grilled, 77, 90
Garlic Dressing, 36
Gorp, 78
Gravy, Cream, 62
Grits, Cheese, 26

Gumbo
  Duck Gumbo, 59
  White Marlin Gumbo, 104

Ham
  Bourbon-Glazed Ham, 118
  Sandwiches, Baked Ham, 28
  Scotch Eggs, 136
Horseradish Dip, Bacon-, 125
Hush Puppies, 61

Ice Cream Cake, 121

Lamb, Pineapple-Mint
  Glazed, 115
Lemon
  Cake, Lemon Pound, 123
  Cake, Lemon Sheet, 127
  Chess Bars, Lemon-Glazed, 90
  Chicken Breasts, Lemon, 18
  Lemonade, Fresh, 123
  Frosting, Lemon Cream, 127
  Parfait, Lemon, 116
  Quail, Lemon-Baked, 50
Lobster Newburg in Patty
  Shells, 111
Lobster-Stuffed Eggs, 111

Marinade, Dill, 114
Marlin
  Barbecued Marlin, 106
  Chowder, Marlin, 104
  Gumbo, White Marlin, 104
  Nuggets, Fried Marlin, 106
Mint Glazed Lamb, Pineapple-, 115
Mint Juleps, 21
Molasses Spice Bars, 17
Mousse, Amaretto, 13
Muffins
  Cornmeal Muffins, 103
  Sour Cream Gems, 26
  Strawberry Muffins, 26
Mushrooms
  Cornbread Dressing,
    Mushroom, 64
  Herbed Mushrooms, 11
  Tomatoes Stuffed with
    Mushrooms, 111

Oatmeal Cake with Coconut
  Topping, 70
Oatmeal Cookies, 136
Onions Baked in Wine, 43
Oranges
  Glaze, Orange, 98
  Juice, Spiced Orange, 77
  Pound Cake, Orange-Glazed
    Pecan, 98
  Relish, Cranberry-Orange, 43
  Sauce, Savory Orange, 31
  Tarts, Orange, 131
  Wine Sauce, Oranges in, 20
Oysters
  Broiled Oysters, 110
  Roasted Oysters, 97
  Slang Jang, 44

Peaches
Bourbon-Blazed Peaches over
Frozen Custard, 93
Bourbon Peaches, 131
Cake, Fresh Peach, 81
Pecans
Cheese Ball, Pecan, 92
Cookies, Pecan Icebox, 23
Pound Cake, Orange-Glazed
Pecan, 98
Petits Fours, Monogrammed, 13
Pheasant aux Fines Herbes, 42
Pies and Pastries
Blackberry Cobbler, Quick, 103
Chocolate Chip Pie, 70
Chocolate Refrigerator Pie, 43
Dewberry Cobbler, 37
Fudge Pie, 127
Fruit Tarts, Glazed, 112
Green Tomato Pie, 68
Meat Pies, Scottish, 134
Orange Tarts, 131
Pumpkin Chiffon Pie, 65
Tart Shells, 112, 131
Pineapple-Mint Glazed Lamb, 115
Pork
Belle Meade Specials, 24
Crackling Cornbread, 78
Sausage Cornbread Sticks, 134
Spareribs, Barbecued, 68
Tenderloins, Pork, 89
Potatoes
Baked Potatoes, Charcoal-, 97
Camp-Style Potatoes, 36
Cheese Potatoes, 55
French-Fried Potatoes, 61
Mashed Potatoes, 64
Salad, Scottish Potato, 136
Salad, Sour Cream Potato, 107
Sweet Potato Buns, 130
Pudding with Bourbon Sauce,
Bread and Butter, 15
Pumpkin Chiffon Pie, 65

Quail
Breakfast Quail, 46
Lemon-Baked Quail, 50
Roast Quail with Savory Orange
Sauce, Cold, 31

Rabbit, Fried, 50
Raspberries, Chilled Custard Sauce
over Strawberries and, 84
Relish, Cranberry-Orange, 43
Relish Salad, Corn, 69
Rice
Confetti Rice, 51
Red Beans and Rice,
Buster's, 133
Salad, Tuna-Rice, 12
Wild Rice and Cheese
Casserole, 42
Rolls and Buns. See also Breads.
Cloverleaf Rolls, 65
Hearty Rolls, 126
Sweet Potato Buns, 130

Salad Dressings
Dill Marinade, 114
French Dressing, 20, 55
Garlic Dressing, 36
Savannah Dressing, 83
Salads
Bean Salad, Cold, 89
Bean Salad, Kidney, 69
Coleslaw, 61, 89
Coleslaw, Almond, 74
Corn Relish Salad, 69
Emerald Salad, 120
Fire and Ice Salad, 65
Fruit Cups, Ginger, 26
Fruit Salad, 78
Garden Salad with French
Dressing, 103
Green Salad with French
Dressing, 55
Layered Salad, Pensacola, 100
Potato Salad, Scottish, 136
Potato Salad, Sour Cream, 107
Roast Beef Salad, Cold, 92
Savannah Salad, 83
Slang Jang, 44
Slaw, Summer, 106
Spinach Mold, 114
Tomato Salad, Marinated, 81
Tossed Salad with Garlic
Dressing, 36
Tuna-Rice Salad, 12
Vegetable Salad, Fresh, 73
Vegetable Salad, Marinated, 20
Vegetable Salad Mold, 111
Vegetables Vinaigrette, 125
Waldorf Salad with Wine, 31
Salmon Spread, Smoky, 129
Sandwiches
Corned Beef Sandwiches, 17
Crab Cake Sandwiches,
Chesapeake Bay, 28
Ham Sandwiches, Baked, 28
Meal-in-a-Sandwich, 74
Pimiento Cheese
Sandwiches, 100
Rolls with Assorted Meats and
Cheeses, Hearty, 126
Shrimp Rolls, 81
Sauces and Gravies
Barbecue Sauce, 72
Barbecue Sauce, Easy, 52
Basting Sauce, 34
Béarnaise Sauce, 24
Bourbon Sauce, 15
Cocktail Sauce, 92
Cocktail Sauce, Spicy, 97
Cream Gravy, 62
Orange Sauce, Savory, 31
Strawberry Sauce over Vanilla Ice
Cream, 56
White Sauce, 47
Sausage Cornbread Sticks, 134
Shortbread Squares, 136
Shrimp
Boiled Shrimp with Cocktail
Sauce, 129
Dill Shrimp, 114
Pickled Shrimp, Chilled, 22
Rolls, Shrimp, 81
Slang Jang, 44
Soups and Stews
Beef Stew, Big-Batch, 78

Broccoli Soup, 18
Burgoo, Old-Fashioned
Kentucky, 15
Chowder, Marlin, 104
Consommé, Herbed Tomato, 31
Cucumber Soup, Cold, 114
Fish Stew, 102
Gumbo, Duck, 59
Gumbo, White Marlin, 104
Ragout of Venison, 40
Squirrel Stew, 51
Sour Cream Gems, 26
Sour Cream Potato Salad, 107
Spinach Balls, 23
Spinach Mold, 114
Squash, Savory Stuffed, 116
Squirrel Stew, 51
Strawberries
Custard Sauce over Strawberries
and Raspberries, Chilled, 84
Muffins, Strawberry, 26
Rich Cream, Strawberries
with, 23
Sauce over Vanilla Ice Cream,
Strawberry, 56
Shortcake, Strawberry, 28
Sweet Potato Buns, 130

Tart Shells, 112, 131
Toast, Texas, 34
Tomatoes
Chutney, Tomato, 47
Consommé, Herbed Tomato, 31
Pie, Green Tomato, 68
Salad, Fire and Ice, 65
Salad, Marinated Tomato, 81
Scalloped Tomatoes,
Parmesan, 51
Stuffed with Mushrooms,
Tomatoes, 111
Tuna-Rice Salad, 12
Turkey
Meal-in-a-Sandwich, 74
Roasted Wild Turkey Breast with
Cream Gravy, 62
Smoked Wild Turkey, 62
Turnips, Creamed, 69

Vegetables
Casserole, Vegetable, 93
Herb Dip with Vegetables, 22
Salad, Fresh Vegetable, 73
Salad, Marinated Vegetable, 20
Salad Mold, Vegetable, 111
Vinaigrette, Vegetables, 125
Venison, Ragout of, 40
Venison Steaks, Barbecued, 52

Waldorf Salad with Wine, 31
Wine
Bars, Wine, 121
Onions Baked in Wine, 43
Sauce, Oranges in Wine, 20
Spritzers, Wine, 116
Waldorf Salad with Wine, 31

Zucchini Bread, 120